A Mother's Touch

Surviving Mother-Daughter Sexual Abuse

JULIE A. BRAND, M.S.

TRAFFORD

USA ▪ Canada ▪ UK ▪ Ireland

Note for Librarians: A cataloguing record for this book is available from Library and Archives
Canada at www.collectionscanada.ca/amicus/index-e.html
ISBN 1-4251-0564-5

TRAFFORD
PUBLISHING™

Offices in Canada, USA, Ireland and UK

Book sales for North America and international:
Trafford Publishing, 6E–2333 Government St.,
Victoria, BC V8T 4P4 CANADA
phone 250 383 6864 (toll-free 1 888 232 4444)
fax 250 383 6804; email to orders@trafford.com
Book sales in Europe:
Trafford Publishing (UK) Limited, 9 Park End Street, 2nd Floor
Oxford, UK OX1 1HH UNITED KINGDOM
phone 44 (0)1865 722 113 (local rate 0845 230 9601)
facsimile 44 (0)1865 722 868; info.uk@trafford.com
Order online at:
trafford.com/06-2322

10 9 8 7 6 5 4 3

Table of Contents

Author's Note

This is a nonfiction work. The incidents and experiences described herein have been faithfully reported as I remembered them. Some names have been changed or, more often, intentionally omitted to protect the privacy of the individuals involved.

Conversations are not necessarily word-for-word from memory or even from my notes. They are intended to be true to the meaning and to the sentiment of the original exchange. Wherever possible, I have sought objective documentation to further substantiate personal recollections.

Chapter 1

The Hand That Rocks The Cradle

MOTHER'S DAY, 1992

"Mother's Day" was a few weeks away. Soon I would be exchanging cards with some of my close women friends who are also moms.

Browsing for cards in a local gift shop felt safe enough on the surface. But I could never be too sure. The card racks overflow with tender emotions and sentimental rhetoric that can melt my carefully crafted armor, leaving me vulnerable again in an instant.

Someone else approached the "Mother's Day" section. She was young—maybe nineteen or so. She glanced around furtively as she took a space next to me. Minutes passed as she pulled out card after card, opening, reading and rejecting each one and placing each back in its designated slot. "This is crazy!" she mumbled, shaking her head and sighing in frustration. A tear slipped down her cheek.

"It's really hard when the words just don't fit her, isn't it?" I ventured. "They all just sound so damn nice."

She looked up at me, startled, as if I'd hit a nerve.

I took a card out and started to read it softly to her. *"You are always there for me, Mom,"* I whispered,... *"with your gentle love and support."* I smiled. "Now that sounds pretty good. It'd be cool

1

to have some of that 'love and support' stuff, huh?"

She nodded, not looking at me.

"Oh, here's a great one," I said, choosing another flowery card to share. *"Mother Dear,"* I read, *"There's just no way to ever thank you enough for all you've done for me through the years."* I paused muttering, "Yeah, right."

Slowly, she leaned over toward me. "I can't seem to find any that fit. None of them sound like her. They all sound so sickeningly sweet. I don't know what to do."

"I know the feeling. It's hard to believe that most people have moms that they can send these cards to, huh? Why weren't we so lucky?"

"Yeah," she nodded. "I think I need to find a card that says, *'Thanks for not hitting me...except when you were drunk.'*"

Now it was my turn to be surprised. "And inside," I added, "It can say, *'But, Mom, you were really drunk a lot!'*"

She burst out laughing. That got us started. Grabbing card after card, we composed more sassy fake lines to share with each other:

"Thanks, Mom, for never being there for me."

"Mom, I'll always remember all your special ways of showing that you didn't care."

"Mom: Why the hell didn't you just get a puppy?"

And, my personal favorite: *"Mother: You are so wrong. **I'm** not the one who needs therapy!"*

We laughed out loud together.

"Oh, gosh, we could develop a whole new line of fractured cards for people from messed up families, huh?" I joked.

"Except we couldn't actually give them to anybody, or they'd kill us!"

Other people stared at us, appearing puzzled by our antics. I wondered if anyone had ever been kicked out of the card shop for inappropriate laughter. We calmed down.

"Hey, seriously, if you really do have to get her a card, I'll help you find one," I offered.

She nodded.

We found a non-schmaltzy, neutral one for her to give. Her mother might have been disappointed, but it would do. It wasn't a card her mother could have shown off to her friends, but neither should it have provoked any serious consequences for the daughter.

We paid for our purchases and headed toward the door.

"Thanks," she offered, seeming a bit embarrassed.

"Me, too," I answered. "Take care."

"You, too," she said, smiling, and we took off in opposite directions.

I wondered how many other people turn away from those mushy cards and go home empty handed. I could only imagine what it would be like to have had one of those gentle greeting card moms.

GOD, MOTHERHOOD AND APPLE PIE

Moms are put on pedestals. All those flowery greeting cards only reinforce our cherished, unwavering beliefs about mothers.

We assume that all mothers are loving and nurturing. Based on what? Do we really think that experiencing pregnancy and childbirth magically transforms every woman (or sixteen-year-old girl) into an empathetic, mature and caring human being? A mother is just a woman who has a baby. There are no required tests or interviews or applications (unless she adopts a child and even then, oops, no mandatory mental-health evaluations needed). The requirements to get a driver's license are more rigorous than to have a child. Why should we presume every mother to be mentally healthy, kind-hearted and safe with kids?

We certainly don't hold that stereotype for males. We don't presume that simply fathering a child transforms men (or sixteen-year-old boys) into non-violent, compassionate, emotionally healthy adults.

Males are suspect for hurting children; females are presumed innocent. If we can't trust mothers to be safe with their children, whom can we trust? As a society, we have a need to believe in the sanctity of motherhood.

But what do we do when mothers kill their young?

Diane Downs killed her children in May of 1983.

Susan Smith drowned her sons in 1994.

Andrea Yates murdered her five young children in 2001.

With the evidence before us, we have to admit our stereotypes were wrong and that the safe boundaries we so carefully drew were just artificial constructs. Then who is to be trusted? Who is the enemy?

David Pelzer (1995) stunned readers with his history of childhood abuse in *A Child Called It*. He was the "black sheep" of his family and his mentally disturbed, alcoholic mother tortured him unmercifully for years.

We need to set aside the motherhood ideal. We know that mental illness exists in the adult female population. We admit that there *are* female sociopaths. Some of these women become mothers. Childbirth is not a cure. Their children are at great risk for being abused. As a society, we must acknowledge that some mothers physically and emotionally abuse their children with beatings and other physical "punishments," threats and humiliations. Sometimes the abuse ends only with the death of the child or of the parent.

We view these mothers as extremely dysfunctional, emotionally disturbed and somehow easily discernible from the average parent you see in the grocery store. We also tend to believe they're very few in number. Certainly they don't live next door to you or attend your church on Sundays or join you on the golf course. Surely the abuse with their children is never sexual.

FEMALE SEXUAL ABUSE PERPETRATORS

Throughout history we have identified men as the "bad guys" when it comes to child sexual abuse. When we learn about fathers who molest, or abusive step-dads, or pedophile priests—whether the victims are male or female—we may too quickly conclude that all sexual abuse perpetrators are males. To think otherwise is just too frightening.

The exposed cases where an adult female has abused an adolescent male (Mary Kay Letourneau's being the most highly publicized) hardly typify female sexual abuse. These cases have been presented in the media as loving and consensual, albeit illegal, because the women's sexual partners were minors. The female perpetrators are treated as interesting and maybe a little strange—mysterious, but hardly vilified. Photos of them with their smiling underage lovers do not scream "abuse" to the average person watching the news. Late-night talk-show hosts jokingly call the boys "lucky" to receive their sexual initiation from attractive adult women. (Jay Leno probably never counseled a confused, suicidal fourteen-year-old boy who had been seduced by a trusted female neighbor.) The media sometimes portrays images that are a far cry from the ugly reality of most child sexual abuse and very different from most abuse that is perpetrated by females.

Male and female sexual abuse perpetrators, acting either independently or together, can sexually abuse children of both genders. Some male perpetrators abuse only girls; others abuse only boys. Some have both male and female victims. Similarly, some female perpetrators abuse only boys; others abuse only girls. Some female child molesters also have victims of both sexes.

Acknowledging that some females do sexually abuse children, we must then expand the traditional list of incest perpetrators to include all female family members as well. Mothers who sexually abuse their own children may, in turn, go on to abuse their grandchildren and their nieces and/or nephews. Neighborhood children may not be safe in their care either.

The following chart lists all possible incest perpetrators and all potential victims of familial sexual abuse.

INCEST: FAMILIAL SEXUAL ABUSE

POSSIBLE PERPETRATORS	POTENTIAL VICTIMS
Father	Daughter
Stepfather	Stepdaughter
Mother *	Son
Stepmother*	Stepson
Grandfather	Granddaughter
Grandmother*	Grandson
Brother	Sister
Stepbrother	Stepsister
Sister*	Brother
Stepsister*	Stepbrother
Female Cousins*	Female Cousins
Male Cousins	Male cousins
Uncle	Niece
Aunt*	Nephew

One half of the potential offenders are female.

Perhaps no greater betrayal exists than mother-child incest. No abuse holds more confusion and shame and guilt for the victims. Given our respect for motherhood and our idealized image of the all-American mom, how are child victims to make any sense out of maternal sexual abuse? Their experiences defy description. And if they could tell, whom would they tell? And what would they say? And who would even believe them?

THE BEST KEPT SECRET: MOTHER-DAUGHTER SEXUAL ABUSE

In the United States, we are reluctant to acknowledge that females ever sexually abuse children, let alone that some women perpetrate against their *own* kids. Maternal incest frequently

6

occurs undetected.

Mother-daughter sexual abuse is especially under-recognized, under-reported and under-researched. To most people, it is simply unthinkable that civilized women would victimize *their own daughters.* Consequently, it is difficult for victims to even find any information about mother-daughter sexual abuse. I know; I tried for years.

Whenever I found a book about sexual abuse, I'd flip to the index, searching for "female perpetrator" and "mother as molester," seeking validation and affirmation that I was not alone. Typical entries read, *"Mothers: as powerless against abusers, as falsely blaming themselves for their husbands' behavior."* Until recently, few authors wrote about mothers who sexually abused their own daughters.

Our cultural denial that mothers can even be perpetrators further isolates victims who predictably may assume that they are the only ones to be so victimized by their own moms. For years, I thought that my childhood was so bizarre and so shameful that no one would ever believe me, let alone understand. I dared not share the "weird" details of my upbringing with anyone for fear of their disgust and rejection.

In 1988, I read in our local newspaper about a support-group meeting for incest survivors. I was finally in counseling and my therapy was progressing well. Here, I thought, was an opportunity to talk with others who had endured childhood experiences similar to mine. I summoned the courage to attend.

I was welcomed into a comfortable setting full of friendly faces, cookies and coffee and smiles. I felt accepted and safe just visiting with the other survivors in the room.

Then it was time to gather at a big table where we were asked to introduce ourselves. One after another, the women identified themselves and their abusers. "Hello, my name is Carol and my perpetrator was my uncle," a young woman said, softly. "My name is Roxanne and my father molested me," offered a middle-aged survivor. "I'm Tina. My older brother abused me," volunteered another. And so it went. Then it was my turn.

"My name is Julie," I said. "I was sexually abused by my mother."

You could have heard the proverbial pin drop. The warm smiles vanished. Women squirmed in their seats. Their once-sympathetic gazes shifted to the floor and the ceiling.

Where had the empathy gone? What had I done or said? In those few awkward moments my mind raced for an answer. I'd revealed just as did the others, but what was the difference? Oh, no! My abuser was the *wrong sex*! I felt like a freak. What was I thinking coming here? I bolted and never went back. Later, someone from the group called to apologize. It didn't matter. I was devastated.

My mother died in 1983, just five days after her sixty-fourth birthday. She died from complications from Creutzfeldt-Jakob Disease, the original, classic form of "mad cow disease."

It is a degenerative brain disorder—always fatal—typically diagnosed in only one in a million people each year. Her death was pain free and quick.

There was a huge funeral with flowers and music and a reception afterwards. Lots of people came to it. Nobody knew our secret.

I was almost 36 years old, and at the funeral while she was being eulogized, try as I might—I couldn't remember a time when I wasn't afraid of her.

Chapter 2

Family Album

HOW I WAS BORN OR
"I WAS AN INDIAN...FOR AWHILE"

My father used to threaten me, "If you don't behave, we'll give you back to the Indians." Evidently, he thought this was a clever form of teasing. Even as an old man, he would laugh, shake his head and say, "I still can't believe you were stupid enough to buy that line." But I *had* believed him. I would dream at night of my people coming to get me. I can still recall that vision: happily riding off into the sunset with my true family, on my very own Pinto, of course.

One day in fourth grade, a girl told me that she was adopted. I had never heard the word before. She was very proud that she had been "chosen." I remember thinking about my dream and my people. I ran home and couldn't wait to tell my parents that it was OK—they could tell me the truth—that I was adopted, too. I had fantasized all day about who my real parents might be. Would they indeed be the Indians my father told me about?

My mother was furious when I asked her if they had adopted me. "Do you know what I went through to have you?" she screamed. Of course, I didn't. I did not know about her difficult pregnancy and childbirth experiences. But I was to learn about them when my father arrived home from work.

That evening my father told the story of the day I was born: October 7, 1947. I was a preemie—born six weeks early and weigh-

9

ing in at only three pounds and fourteen ounces. Many babies that small did not make it. They didn't think I would. Even then, I was a survivor.

I was born at a military hospital at Camp Lejeune, North Carolina, where my father was stationed with the Marine Corps. "We thought you were already dead," my father would say, repeating the story almost verbatim each time. "The doctor could not get a heartbeat for you. Your poor mother was so sick with toxemia, I was afraid I'd lose her. The doctor cut her open to get you out and save her. I was waiting in the hallway when the doctor suddenly came out holding this bloody thing in his hands. That was you! The doctor called out to me, 'It's alive!' and ran down the hall to find an incubator. I have to tell you, I really didn't care about you at all then. All I cared about was if your mother was going to be ok. You almost killed your mother, you know—I never would have forgiven you if you'd lived and she'd died."

The story was told over and over throughout my childhood. His words were seared in my memory—"already dead...this bloody thing... it's alive...I really didn't care about you...I never would never have forgiven you." I knew them by heart.

For my first six weeks, according to my father, my world was an incubator at the hospital. When I did finally come home, neighbors and friends on the military base had to take care of me; my mother was too sick with complications from the Caesarian surgery. She often used to say, "Maybe the reason you're so damn independent is that you lived in an incubator for so long." As if I'd had a choice?

Years later, I would tell a therapist that I constantly heard myself apologizing to other people. Often its essence was, "Hello, my name is Julie. I'm sorry."

"What do you feel so guilty about? What was your crime?"

It comes as no surprise now that I quickly answered, "Being born."

No Witnesses

Nobody knows what really goes on within a home except the family members who live there. As an only child, I had no one to bear witness to my mother's bizarre behavior or to help me challenge my parents' rules and beliefs. No one was there to look at across the room and silently mouth, "Did you hear what she just said? She's wacko!"

My relatives lived far away in other states. Occasionally a few, like my grandpa or my great aunt, came for short visits. Mother was a skilled actress. She played to her audience. She would behave so nicely for the benefit of others that I hardly recognized her. Yet as young as I was, I was able to determine from the difference in her demeanor that she *knew* how she was supposed to conduct herself as a mother.

With no one else around, things were very different. "Wipe that expression off your face right now, young lady!" my mother would hiss, if I dared to even show my unhappiness over a new rule or punishment. When I was hardly ever allowed to go to friends' houses to play, I accepted that it was "for my own good." When my pet turtles mysteriously died while I was at school, I believed my mother's feeble explanations and did not complain. When I had to get undressed and lie down for "nap time with Mommy," I acquiesced every time.

I never dared to talk back to either of my parents. I was submissive, compliant, obedient and usually even cheerful in my demeanor. I was also scared to death.

I was afraid of a God who would punish me for my multiple sins. I tried to make sense out of the conflicting stories that mother told me. She said, "God loves children." But then she also told me, "He is watching you every minute to see if you make any mistakes." We're not talking about stealing or hurting other kids; my mother's God was into good manners and social graces. "He has rules, young lady. For example, if you pick your nose He might choose to freeze your hand right there forever—freeze you in the act—and the whole world will know the bad thing you did."

She also warned me, "If you ever touch yourself 'down there,' God could freeze your hand there forever." (Later I would struggle to understand why it was permissible for *her* to touch me "down there"—on my "privates"—during our "nap time" but if I ever dared touch myself, God might surely zap me.)

What I imagined God could do to a nine-year-old little girl was not a pretty picture! I envisioned walking around forever with one finger up my nose and my other hand rubbing my crotch for the whole world to see. I was horrified. OK, like most kids, it never stopped me from picking my nose or masturbating but it was frightening. I just hoped that God was far too busy monitoring other sinners to see me.

I was also afraid of my father. He would spank me with a yardstick or ruler for things I did wrong. I got hit for little stupid things, like not drinking all my milk at dinnertime. He always followed her orders. Sometimes he punished me for infractions that my mother totally made up. He believed everything and anything she said. He may have been the career Marine, but my mother was the boss in our house. Her word was law.

When I turned sixteen, I wanted to take a driver's education class in school. It seemed like a reasonable request. Mother said, "You're too immature to drive a car. You'll just get in an accident. And anyway, we're not paying for your car insurance so that's that." I didn't protest and I didn't stomp out. Even in high school, I still knew not to cross her. But I also didn't drive until years later, after I was married and had a child. Driving took independence and confidence and a parental release form. I had none of those.

People who grow up in emotionally healthy families find it extremely difficult to understand how a parent can have such total control over a teenager. My adult daughter can't grasp it. "*I* wouldn't have just stood there and taken it, Mom. I'd have told her off and walked out!" How can she possibly understand my fear-based childhood when she grew up respected and celebrated?

I always knew not to defy my mother, especially when she would give me "the look." She'd clench her jaw and her eyes would go cold. Even back when I couldn't remember exactly what it was she could do to me, I knew it wasn't good.

Turns out, I was right to be afraid.

IN THE KITCHEN WITH MOMMY

The story about the kitchen and the oven is told here not to shock or to elicit sympathy, but to characterize the level of psychological control my mother had over me throughout her lifetime. It explains why I felt so helpless in her clutches.

I would not recall what happened in the kitchen until decades later, after my mother had died. Then I began experiencing flashbacks to specific incidents from my childhood. I no longer had to be afraid of her; she could not hurt me from the grave.

What happened that fateful day in Quantico, Virginia, back in 1949 would underscore my relationship with my mother for all time. What she did would sentence me to a childhood of fear and submission and silence me from telling anyone about the sexual abuse still to come.

Mother did not like messes. Toddlers make messes when they are allowed to play—with water, sand, dirt, crayons. I was not allowed to make messes. But toddlers also make messes in their diapers. It is normal and natural for even the most well behaved, compliant, sweet little eighteen-month-old girl to still accidentally poop her pants. I did not deserve what came next.

Mother and I were alone in the kitchen. I can picture the large black and white squares of linoleum on the floor. There was a stove with glass on the front oven door.

I was standing in the kitchen, wearing just a diaper. Maybe she had just changed my diaper five minutes before. I don't know. What I do know is that she leaned down and checked my diaper and I had messed again. She went ballistic with rage—screaming and grabbing me. She took both of my hands, flattening them out, pressing them and holding them against the hot glass. I screamed with pain.

It wasn't until 1988 that I had "the kitchen remembrance." I did not want to believe it. I telephoned my father and bombarded him with questions, hoping that he would refute my latest childhood memory. But the information that I obtained from him only substantiated my worst fears.

Trying to sound casual, I asked whether or not I had ever been burned as a child. He quickly answered, "Of course, you were. Don't you remember? Umm... I suppose we never talked about it later on."

"Was I just little?" I asked him. "What happened, Dad?"

He asked, "Don't you remember the bandages? You were just a baby...maybe seventeen or eighteen months old...You had second-degree burns on both your hands. Your little hands had to be bandaged for weeks...I remember how you hated that."

Then came the most unnerving words of all. "I never knew exactly what happened. I was at work. Your mother called me, frantic...I went home and got you and we took you to the doctor. Somehow you had gotten burned. I don't recall what she said happened."

On the phone, my father was actually rather blasé about the whole thing. I suppose he never asked and I'm sure he never investigated. He trusted her blindly. After all, if you can't trust your wife, whom can you trust?

I had finally learned why I had always been scared to death of her. I wasn't crazy; I had been one smart little kid. I knew that mother could hurt me very badly. She had done it before and no one, not even my father, could stop her. Mother was all-powerful. I had decided that I would comply with whatever she said from then on. She owned me.

In 1999, I came home to help move my father from his house of 36 years into an assisted-living residence. Sorting through the family bookcase, I found my ancient faded pink baby book entitled *Baby's Own Story*, along with my mother's high school yearbook and her bride's "memory book." Inside the back cover of my baby book, my mother had recorded the dates of my illnesses and immunizations.

In her distinctive handwriting, my mother had written:

"April, 1949—Hand burns, dysentery"

The two entries were linked that fateful day.
The trepidation I had felt throughout childhood and even during my adolescence was not irrational. Now I knew why I had always feared displeasing her, even in adulthood. She was someone who, when crossed, could and would inflict pain.

PIECES OF THE PUZZLE

Working with my childhood memories has been a lot like tackling a complicated jigsaw puzzle. I have many isolated pieces of the puzzle—colorful and vivid—but I am not sure where and how to fit them into the whole picture of my childhood. I don't know exactly where they belong.

For example, I remember having a "Princess Margaret" Madame Alexander doll. I can clearly see her flawless porcelain face, her pale rose-colored dress and her perfect lacquered hair. But I don't recall who gave her to me or when or where. I remember mother saying the doll was "too good" for me to play with so she stood covered in plastic in a stand on my dresser. I was allowed to take her down and hold her from time to time but only under mother's watchful eye. I ached to play with her—to dress her and to comb her hair—but I never dared. I did not want to risk my mother's wrath.

I can recall a motel-size swimming pool and my father standing in water, mid-chest, calling for me to jump off the side to him. His arms were extended to catch me and I would not do it. He became angry; I had refused an order. But I just couldn't do it. I did not trust him to be able to save me. Where were we? (San Diego? Palm Springs?) How that piece fits with all the others, I do not know.

For many years, I had virtually no memory of my childhood before the age of nine. This is in stark contrast to normal, sequential memories, both positive and negative, from fourth grade to the present.

Logic dictates I was enrolled in school. Records prove that I actually attended kindergarten in Oceanside, California. I look at an old black and white group photo of my kindergarten class. I know which girl is supposed to be me. I look rather demure and sweet but it could be anybody. I can't get into her skin. I have no recollection of my classroom teacher or activities or the friends I had or didn't have.

My adult children can still remember various birthday parties they had as kids; I can't. I turned five and six and seven and eight but I remember no parties, gifts, or celebrations. I have seen old photos of me with a bicycle with training wheels—another piece of the mosaic. I still don't remember it. I don't identify at all with the child in the picture.

Who was I? The only concrete clues to those years are found in my old report cards. It appears that I was a sweet, friendly, well-behaved little girl. But for three years—from kindergarten through second grade—three different teachers expressed some concerns about my emotional development in their "teacher comments" section.

In 1953, Mrs. Helen Crumley was my kindergarten teacher in Oceanside, California. She wrote:

> Julie is a fine little Kg. and I enjoy her very much. She is cooperative & well liked by her little classmates and most anxious to follow all directions. Gets upset easily though when she thinks things are not quite right. When I assure her that all is well she responds readily and is happy again. Is she sensitive at home too? Or perhaps because we are all still new to her at school? (San Diego County Schools "Report to Parents," Kindergarten 1952-1953, South Oceanside School, Appendix A.)

My mother's parental response:

> Mrs. Crumley-

> Yes, Julie is very sensitive at home but as you say, easily reassured if she thinks something is not quite right. She's in her glory when she is in large groups and really seems happy and confident most of the time. Her sensitivity shows itself, too, in nightly dreams and frequent nightmares. If any problems do arise we'll be more than happy to cooperate in

any way. Please feel free to call on us. (San Diego County Schools "Report to Parents," Kindergarten 1952-1953, South Oceanside School, Appendix A.)

My first grade teacher, Dorothy Childers, noted similar concerns:

Julia is a very quite [sic], good girl. She is sometimes a little nervous, but is doing good work. (San Diego City Schools "Primary Pupil Growth Report," Grade One 1953-1954, Will Angier School, Appendix A.)

My mother again responded:

We're happy Julie is doing well. If there is anything we can do to help in her growth, let us know. We haven't noticed the nervousness but she is very sensitive and aware of others. She comes home with her woes, we explain the "whys & wherefore" and she's happy again. (San Diego City Schools "Primary Pupil Growth Report," Grade One 1953-1954, Will Angier School, Appendix A.)

For second grade the report card indicates that I had Mrs. Ponder. (I still don't recall any of these teachers.) For the second "teacher's message" of three such reports during the year, the teacher wrote:

Julia is continuing her good work. She has a sweet personality and is very dependable. Sometimes I feel she gets very nervous if everything isn't just 'perfect.' Perhaps you can help her in reading. I believe she needs more confidence, also expression. (San Diego City Schools "Primary Pupil Growth Report," Grade 2, 1954-1955, Grantville School, Appendix A.)

The parental response is in my father's handwriting this time. But it does not sound like him at all. I suspect my mother wrote out the correct response and then had him copy it on the report card so they could demonstrate that both mother and father were involved in my education:

We are very pleased with Julia's report. Will follow your suggestion to assist Julia in her reading development. We too have noted a bit of nervousness, but she appears to be outgrowing it. (San Diego City Schools "Primary Pupil Growth Report," Grade 2, 1954-1955, Grantville School, Appendix A.)

Teachers were concerned that I was "nervous." In first grade my mother had written that they did not see any nervousness at home. In second grade my father wrote that they had "noted a bit of nervousness" but that I was outgrowing it. Interesting. To me "nervous" means anxious, apprehensive and uneasy. That fits. I had reasons to be nervous, given my family.

When my mother died in 1983, I was immediately flooded with different vignettes from my childhood—new puzzle pieces. Many were innocuous little recollections: a Brownie troop meeting where the leader was holding her new baby; a day at the Oregon coast with my grandfather and parents; having the measles and lying on a couch under a black crocheted blanket with squares of colorful flowers. Others were perplexing flashes to bizarre and frightening feelings or incidents, always alone with my mother. Over time, with ever-increasingly clear recall and with external collaboration, I have filled in some of the blanks of my past.

I have always remembered our house in San Diego. It was pink stucco and on a corner up a hill. We had something called "ice plant" growing in up the hillside in the backyard. It had a new redwood fence with multiple gates. My friend, Charlie, and I played cowboys and hid behind the open gates, "shooting" at each other—making the sound effects with our toy guns. That was great fun!

I always remembered my bedroom in fourth grade. I had a maple finish double bed with a bookcase headboard and an ugly dark brown bedspread. How I ended up with such an ugly bedspread, I do not know. But I know that I was supposed to be happy and grateful. "Aren't you lucky to have such a big bed?" my mother would say. "I'll bet your little friends just have twin beds." The real reason I got to have a double bed: so there was room for my mother to lie down with me for our "nap time."

You would think that everyone would have some happy

Christmas holiday childhood memories. I have wracked my brain, but they just aren't forthcoming. I remember my fourth grade Christmas. It was the last Christmas I would believe in Santa Claus. Charlie told me the truth soon afterwards.

Mother coordinated the decorating of the Christmas tree. It was very important to her that it was done perfectly. She conducted the tree-trimming activity as though some home decorating magazine crew (we had no Martha Stewart television program back then) was coming to inspect her handiwork.

She individually placed each ornament on the tree herself or told my father *exactly* where to place them, following some imagined pattern of ideal assigned slots. No spontaneity was allowed. I don't remember my ever choosing or placing a single ornament. If I ever made an ornament at school, it certainly would not have been judged as good enough to go on *her* tree.

She loved tinsel, but it had to be put on the tree *correctly*. "A job worth doing is worth doing well, young lady!" One strand at a time, evenly spaced and hanging uniformly over the tree branches. What do you think the chances are of a highly scrutinized, nervous nine-year-old kid applying the tinsel properly? She would always blow up over it. "Can't you do anything right? I just showed you how to do it! You just don't care. You are messing it up on purpose. Go to your room, Missy. I'll just do it all over myself!"

The weeks just before Christmas my father repeatedly taunted me, "Do you really think Santa will bring *you* anything? Do you honestly think you have been a good girl?" Well, I had thought so but now I didn't know. I reviewed a litany of recent misbehaviors. I had cried a couple of times, I had a messy room, I forgot to make my bed and I wasn't in the top fourth grade reading group. The list seemed endless. I didn't have a prayer.

"I hear that Santa leaves coal in the stockings of the bad little girls," he said, frowning. How was I to know that this was his idea of teasing? If your own father questions your worthiness, maybe you really don't deserve anything. After all, "Father Knows Best." My dad loved to endlessly quote the title of that television show, as though his saying so made it fact.

I remember sneaking out Christmas morning to see the tree before anyone else awakened. Tiptoeing into the living room, I was so relieved to see some gift tags bearing my name. Whew! I did get some presents from Santa. I would not have to face the humiliation of knowing that Santa Claus had judged me undeserving.

Christmas morning was not fun. Mother controlled everything. She stalled and came out from their bedroom later than usual. Then my father muttered, "Umm, Santa must have thought you were OK after all," shrugging his shoulders. Next, I was allowed to open my stocking, pausing to pose for required photos.

A mandatory, atypical, long drawn out breakfast of eggs and French toast and bacon came next. We finally finished eating and mother said, "Not yet, Julie, we adults have the right to another cup of coffee." I swear that she stretched it out endlessly, on purpose. Finally, she would announce that it was time to go back into the living room to open our presents.

The opening of the gifts was orchestrated also. As the only child, it was my job to distribute all the presents to everyone until the Christmas tree skirt was naked. We each sat in our designated seats with our pile of gifts at our feet. Then my mother ("ladies first") would open all of her presents—slowly and methodically writing down the gifts and the givers' names on a notepad and holding up the larger presents for photographs. Next it was my father's turn. She passed him the scissors and the notepad and pen. She took the staged pictures of him opening his gifts. Finally, around eleven o'clock Christmas morning, at last it was my turn. After each gift was opened, I would have to stop to write down the present and the giver in the neat columns that would compose my "thank you" list. I smiled and carefully expressed grateful and humble thanks for each present.

Afterwards, it was my job to carefully arrange all the opened gifts back under the tree. I assume this was done to have them on display just in case any friends or neighbors should drop by later. I don't remember any of my parents' friends or neighbors ever just stopping by to visit us—certainly not coming into the house.

Then it was time to go to my room to write my thank you notes.

Mother would, of course, inspect each letter for appropriate length, correct spelling and grammar and witty prose. If not acceptable, I would have to re-do them. Only after completing my thank you notes to her satisfaction, could I play with my Christmas toys.

If my father found these Christmas day procedures to be joy-less or downright weird, he never protested. But then, I do not remember him *ever*, in his ninety years on the planet, standing up to her or taking my side about anything. Not once.

When I was in my twenties, from time to time my mother would question me, "You really don't remember anything from when you were little?"

"Nothing much before fourth grade," I would reply.

"Oh, well. You and I were so close and we had such happy times together. You probably don't remember because it was just girl fun—just fluff."

But I knew it *wasn't* fun and it wasn't "just fluff." Fluff doesn't scare the hell out of you.

Chapter 3

Abuse Facts & Stats

DO WE REALLY CARE ABOUT KIDS?

Child abuse has not always been against the law in the United States. We appear to be so compassionate towards children when we speak out against child trafficking in India or child rape in South Africa or against the American stores that buy and sell clothing made by children laboring in foreign sweatshops. Yet, it may surprise many people that we passed laws in this country to protect our animals from being abused more than one hundred years *before* we had any federal laws to protect our children.

The American Society for the Prevention of Cruelty to Animals was founded in 1866. Soon after, the New York State legislature passed the first laws against animal cruelty in the United States. It granted the ASPCA the right to investigate and to arrest citizens who broke animal-abuse laws. At that time, children had no similar protection. (ASPCA web site)

In contrast, "The Federal Child Abuse Prevention and Treatment Act" (CAPTA) was not passed until 1974. Some states developed their own protective organizations and laws earlier than 1974 and New York again took the lead. The New York Society for the Prevention of Cruelty to Children (NYSPCC) was formed in 1875 and worked closely with New York law enforcement agencies by creating a statewide system for reporting and documenting child abuse. The NYSPCC agency worked diligently to pass state laws mandating the investigation and prosecution of child-abuse cases. New York's state laws regarding the welfare and treatment of children became the model for other states and the basis for eventual federal legislation. (NYSPCC web site)

Why were we (and why are we still) so slow to take action on the behalf of our nation's children? How can it be "politically correct" to appear to care about children's issues while simultaneously slashing federal and state budgets for social and mental health services. Why isn't *preventing* child abuse a top priority in this country?

I think there are multiple reasons why we have not effectively addressed the problem of child abuse during the last thirty years:

1) *Denial.* If we can distance ourselves from the abuse, it is easier to maintain our disbelief. We tell ourselves that it rarely happens and when it does, it happens to "other people"—to people we don't know. We make assumptions about the social class, ethnicity and gender of both the victims and the perpetrators, thus creating false stereotypes that artificially separate "them" from "us."

In reality, child abuse happens in *all* kinds of families across all socio-economic levels, ethnic backgrounds and education levels. A family dentist might beat his sons; the local minister could be molesting his two daughters. An elementary school principal could be touching children inappropriately in her office. As a society we need to get past our comfortable state of denial. Child abuse frequently happens to victims and by perpetrators whom you might never suspect.

2) *Child abuse is unpleasant to consider.* Non-offending, safe adults do not like to even think about children being hurt—emotionally, physically, or sexually. It makes them feel angry and fearful and helpless. When something causes us to have unpleasant feelings, the quickest fix is simply not to think about it.

Sexual abuse, particularly incest, is perhaps the most difficult type of abuse for many people to imagine. I have come to accurately anticipate the responses I'll receive when I disclose about my own abuse. The listeners' facial expressions scream out "Yuck!"

and "Gross!" Sometimes the very people who seemed comfortable interacting with me just seconds before, now seek a quick retreat. I understand. I don't blame them. But if healthy, safe, never-victimized adults can't even bear to discuss parent-child sexual abuse, how on Earth can we expect the fragile child victims themselves to tell the authorities about their incest experiences?

Adult survivors exist in all walks of life. Some who are in positions of power in our government may be unable to speak out because they still carry their own unresolved victimization issues. The subject matter may be "too close to home" and too threatening. Many with influence and authority may not be just bystanders—they could be victims themselves, or perpetrators, or have family members who fall into both categories. Identifying oneself as a victim or as a perpetrator is so shame-based that many victims and abusers never get the therapeutic help they need.

3) *We are afraid of falsely accusing anyone of child abuse.* People report other suspected crimes to the police so that law enforcement personnel can investigate and make arrests if warranted. Suspects of other crimes may be initially accused of wrong doing and then subsequently cleared.

But with child abuse, the person who is reporting often feels that he or she must provide proof and conduct an ironclad investigation *before* ever calling Social Services or the Police Department. Even mandated reporters such as school teachers, counselors and nurses sometimes hesitate to call in suspected abuse because they are not "sure." Maybe they find it impossible to believe that Mr. Jones, a "pillar of the community," would hurt his children or perhaps they are afraid that the identified parents will be angry with them.

A middle-school girl once told me that her father had been beating her. She had no marks or bruises but more significantly, she showed little emotion. She described the recent incident with her father, slowly and precisely, as though well rehearsed. But, I still reported the case to Social Services. I explained to the social worker why I was skeptical of the young woman's story—her lack of affect, the open communication and healthy relationship she had described with her parents up to this time—*but I still made the report.* My job was not to investigate and not to determine whether the accused parent was guilty or innocent. My responsibility was to report.

The girl later admitted to a Social Services caseworker that she made up the story in retaliation for being grounded. Her parents were exonerated. The next day I phoned the parents. I explained that I was the person who had made the report and my legal responsibility to report all suspected abuse. They understood. They were not angry with me for doing my job nor were they defensive. Most of all, they were concerned about their daughter and getting her the professional help she needed.

All non-offending parents should be open to questioning and scrutiny. No exceptions. When my own daughter was about five or six, she was exceptionally active. Those years we made numerous trips with her to the emergency room. She was injured trying to play croquet; she somehow cut her chin on the ice at the public ice rink. She had stitches three different times in the same specific spot on her chin. During one of these unscheduled hospital visits, I actually suggested to the young ER physician that maybe he would like to take her alone into another room to ask her what happened. I said something such as, "We have been in here a lot lately. I would understand if you suspected abuse. Please feel free to talk with her alone to hear her explanation of the injuries." I meant it. I had nothing to hide. I wanted him to be observant and suspicious. He declined.

4) *We place supreme value on respecting the privacy of families.* Why? According to the most recent child maltreatment national statistics, *eighty per cent of all child abuse perpetrators were the parents of the victims.* ("Child Maltreatment 2003: Summary of Key Findings") Yet we don't want to question what is going on behind the closed doors of the typical American family. We never want to be rude and we certainly don't mean to imply that anything might be wrong. In spite of the facts, we continue to presume that being a parent somehow makes a person an innocent and healthy caregiver.

Just whom are we protecting here? Are we choosing to protect the adults' reputations over the children's lives? Who pays the price?

It should come as no surprise that most children who are sexually abused by their own parents never tell anyone; their cases are typically not even included in our statistics. They don't tell because they don't trust that anyone is powerful enough to help them—more powerful than their mother or father. They don't trust that they will be believed. Often they are right. If a victim tells and there is no rescue, it may only make it worse for the child. Taking a chance and telling the authorities could mean more abuse. It could even lead to death.

5) *Prevention programs focus on children.* Do we really expect children to be able to protect themselves? Many abuse education programs, especially those designed to prevent sexual abuse, seem to make children responsible for their own safety.

In the early 1990's, I taught a "Sexual Abuse Prevention" curriculum in my middle school. With sixth graders, I used a professionally produced VHS tape containing a series of vignettes of potentially dangerous situations. Child actors demonstrated how to identify the danger signs in each scenario. Using these simulated examples, I basically taught twelve-year-olds that *they* should be able to assess their own safety in various settings, get away from any dangerous persons or activities and immediately go tell someone. Did we unintentionally communicate that if they were victimized then they had not followed the steps correctly and it was *their* fault? Those particular steps are likely to only be effective in some situations of stranger or acquaintance abuse. We must make it clear that it is *never the child's fault*—not when the abuser is a total stranger and not even when the perpetrator is a trusted and loved member of the family, even a parent or grandparent.

Abuse-prevention programs should also be targeting young adults in their twenties. We need to reach out to and intervene with young men and young women before they have children and certainly before they have the opportunity to harm their own kids.

Where are the policy makers? Who is developing a national agenda that embraces the welfare of our children? *Why are we not intervening with all new parents before they abuse?* Why not offer free parenting classes, support groups and home-visitation programs through every hospital and birthing center in the country? Some communities do offer these types of programs, but most don't and very few offer all three components at no cost to the participants.

Why don't we make it the norm—the "in thing" for new parents? Buy the car seat, have the baby shower, attend "Healthy Parenting" classes and meet your "Home Visitor." And in those classes, let's *talk* about different parenting styles and what is emotionally safe childrearing and what is abusive. Let's teach new parents loving, responsible ways to discipline their children. Let's gear the program for *all* parents—not just college students who have already taken numerous child development classes or "at risk" teenage parents. Let's talk about risk factors (because everyone has them) whether for medical conditions such as diabetes or for genetic predispositions such as alcoholism or for learned dysfunctional behavior such as physical abuse. Take away the shame and the blame and, let's problem solve together!

All adults have their "lists" from their own childhoods—the verbal and/or written lists of "things that my parents did to me that I swear I will never do to my kids." The lists might have items such as, "make me eat broccoli" or "wear fancy clothes to church" or "take my younger sister everywhere with me." Other adults' lists might say not to "hit, swear at, put down, embarrass, punch, humiliate, yell, molest, beat or ridicule." But everybody—including my own adult children and step-children—everybody has a list.

Why don't we just admit, "Hey, it **is** extremely challenging and difficult being a parent and we need to work together and help each other. All parents want the best for their kids and our community wants every child to grow up feeling safe and loved. We believe parents can be helped to make safe, non-violent choices about how they raise their kids."

Why don't we talk about parenting as much as we talk about football? Why don't we make caring for our kids as important as caring for our cars or even our front lawns? Why don't we say, "There are some things I want to do differently with my own kids" and then consciously do them?

6) *We don't genuinely believe that child abuse is preventable.* I *know* the cycle of abuse can be broken because I broke it in my family. (Oh, I made tons of mistakes. I sometimes yelled. I was frustrated by what were just normal sibling arguments, but my kids were never abused physically, emotionally or sexually.) I *know* it is preventable. People who have grown up with personal violence and abuse **can** learn new constructive ways of interacting with their own children.

Focusing on the negative is easy. Maybe you have seen the statistics about the high percentages of prison inmates that suffered from childhood abuse. Research studies have connected adult women's dependence on illegal drugs with a high incidence of childhood sexual abuse; women who experienced physical abuse in childhood have higher rates of domestic violence in their adult lives. It makes sense.

But does anyone ever survey safe, non-violent, non-abusive adults to find out what percent of them were abused as kids? Do we survey PTA presidents or librarians or physicians or U.S. Congressmen or chemical engineers (or school counselors) to find out what percent of them were maltreated? I would be interested in learning what percent of these groups report childhood abuse. What percent have broken the pattern with their own kids? How did they accomplish this?

In Chapter Nine we'll discuss some prevention ideas that may help to create and to support healthy, safe families. Rather than instantly condemning, judging and shaming adults, we need to work with parents who are at risk for harming their children and offer to show them alternative ways of interacting with their kids.

No Children Left Behind

Educators working in our schools—"in the trenches"—see the challenges facing our nation's children every day: poverty, profound neglect, abuse and violence. They see our kids turn to alcohol and other drugs, self-injury, sex, juvenile delinquency, gangs and violent crime in futile attempts to cope with the pain and chaos. While good schools are havens of safety and support for kids, alone they can never be enough.

'I was on the National Commission for Children and Families and we went around the country looking at what was happening to families and children. And we found that we're the least child- and family-oriented society in the civilized world. And we also saw the price that we're paying: angry, contained, unavailable children who can't learn.'

(Dr. T. Berry Brazelton, M.D., Professor Emeritus of Pediatrics, Harvard Medical School, Healthy Families America web site)

This quote only echoes what teachers, social workers and school counselors have known for years. Yet the authors of "No Child Left Behind," the guidelines for national school accountability, seem unaware of the social problems facing today's children. If a child is worried about being hit (*or "hit on"*) nightly at home or not having enough food to eat, then completing homework is just not a very high priority. Neither is performing well on some education bureaucrats' standardized tests.

I remember the years after Colorado initiated its mandatory CSAP testing (Colorado Student Assessment Program) in order to meet the standardized statewide testing requirements of NCLB. I was a middle school counselor working with sixth through eighth grade students; they ranged in age from eleven to fourteen. Two of my female students—bright, academically solid young women—did not attend school on the first day of the CSAP testing. Didn't they know how important this was? Didn't they feel a moral obligation to do their best?

If the girls didn't take the test, they would receive zeroes *and* those zeroes would lower our school's overall scores. We would all be shamed by the comparisons to other middle schools' scores published on the front page the local newspaper; our dedicated teachers would be publicly chastised in the "Letters to the Editor" section. The Accountability Committee would place us "on watch" as a "low performing school" and we might be given just three years to improve or be taken over by a private company! So, dang it, why didn't these girls just come to school?

Because they were sexually assaulted the weekend before the testing. Victims of violent crimes, both girls missed two weeks of school as they worked with law-enforcement personnel and received counseling services. Their mothers were highly supportive of them, thank goodness. Their mothers no longer cared at all about the dang CSAP testing.

A few days later, I naively e-mailed our school district's testing coordinator to ask what code I should mark to excuse these girls from their standardized testing. I was told that there were no excuses and no special categories. The girls each received zeroes. No code existed for "Personal trauma" or "Family emergency" or even a "Medical emergency." So if a girl was raped or a boy's mother was killed in a car accident the night before testing or a boy's father left belt-buckle impressions imbedded in his forehead—too bad but no exceptions. "Life is hard—deal with it and you'd better show up for testing tomorrow." This is the implicit message that child victims receive from their schools, their states and their country's leaders.

There are two major sources of information about the victims of child abuse and their perpetrators:

1) Government statistics (which document only those cases actually reported to and investigated by social service agencies)

2) Research studies in which adults complete anonymous "retrospective surveys" indicating the specific abusive behaviors that they experienced during their childhoods and identify-

ing their sexual abuse perpetrators.

Analysis of such child sexual abuse statistics and studies leads to the conservative estimate that approximately twenty percent of females and five to ten percent of males are sexually abused (with or without actual physical contact) before the age of eighteen. (Finkelhor, 1994, p. 37) *This translates to one out of every five girls and one in every ten to twenty boys will be sexually abused during their childhoods.* In a typical middle school class of fifteen girls and fifteen boys, three girls and one boy are likely to be victimized. For the sake of our schools' standardized testing results, let's just hope that it somehow doesn't happen during their schools' designated testing weeks. After all, we have our priorities.

How can anyone still be in denial about the social and family problems facing today's youth? We have hundreds of thousands of children just struggling to survive their brutal childhoods in the United States of America *today.* Of course a lot of those kids are not performing well on standardized tests. Where did we ever get the idea that a high-quality academic program at school could totally compensate for a low-quality, violent life experience at home?

THE CASE OF "MARY ELLEN"

During the 1990's I taught several graduate courses about child abuse to teachers and other education specialists. Although I never told my own personal story, I would say something like, "Many of us who grew up in dysfunctional families learned to... ." Including myself in this casual way helped any of the audience members, who also happened to be survivors, to feel acknowledged and safe. By the end of each course, some participants had shared that they, too, were survivors of childhood abuse.

During the first class session I always told them the story of "Mary Ellen." Until this little girl's tragic suffering was well publicized, most people were unaware of the severity and frequency of child abuse. Her story, and the courageous actions of the individuals who helped her, led to the development of The New York

Society for the Prevention of Cruelty to Children. ("The Real Story of Mary Ellen Wilson," American Humane web site)

Mary Ellen Wilson was born in 1864 to a married couple in New York. Her father died shortly after her birth and her mother found it increasingly difficult to support herself and the child. Her mother paid another woman to care for Mary Ellen. When the payments and the visits stopped, that caregiver turned the child over to the city's "Department of Charities." Mary Ellen was two years old at that time. The city placed her with Mary and Thomas McCormack. Not long after they got Mary Ellen, Mr. McCormack died. His widow married a Mr. Francis Connolly and together with Mary Ellen, they moved into a tenement apartment building.

Their neighbors were concerned about the child. One of them asked Etta Wheeler, a Methodist outreach worker, who often visited the poor tenement residents to check on Mary Ellen. Etta followed up on the family even though they had moved to a different apartment. A neighbor there heard crying. Etta found an excuse to meet Mrs. Connolly and got to see little Mary Ellen. She was now ten years old—thin, dirty, with scars and bruises on her arms and legs. Her clothing was threadbare.

Etta went to Henry Bergh for help. He was a leader in the animal rights movement and just eight years earlier, he had started the American Society for the Prevention of Cruelty to Animals (ASPCA). She took him written statements from neighbors who were willing to testify that Mary Ellen was being abused. He got a NYSPCA investigator to pose as a census taker to get inside the apartment and confirm the neighbors' descriptions. Mr. Bergh was acting as a concerned, private citizen, but it was his connections with city government, law enforcement and the press that made the intervention successful.

Reporters from the *New York Times* covered the story as Mary Ellen testified in court. This fragile little girl told of daily beatings with a twisted whip and black and blue marks and of her "mother" striking her with a pair of scissors. The judge placed her under the protective guardianship of the court. Major newspapers covered the trial of Mary Connolly. On April 21, 1874 she was found guilty of felonious assault and sentenced to one year of hard labor in prison.

Mary Ellen was placed in loving foster homes, with relatives of Etta Wheeler. Ellen's own children and grandchildren described her as "gentle and not much of a disciplinarian." She died in 1956 at the age of ninety-two. (American Humane web site)

Publicity from Mary Ellen's case increased the public's awareness of child abuse and gave local New York agencies the power to speak out. They advocated for the existing state laws to be enforced and for new laws to be written to better protect children.

On Tuesday, April 27, 1875, The New York Society for the Prevention of Cruelty to Children—the first child protection agency in the world—was incorporated. John D. Wright, another respected New York philanthropist, served as its first president. Henry Bergh and Elbridge Gerry were named vice-presidents.

The organization's unique purpose was:

'to rescue little children from the cruelty and demoralization which neglect, abandonment and improper treatment engender; to aid by all lawful means in the enforcement of the laws intended for their protection and benefit; to secure by like means the prompt conviction and punishment of all persons violating such laws and especially such persons as cruelly ill treat and shamefully neglect such little children of whom they claim the care, custody or control.'

("The Response," The New York Society for the Prevention of Cruelty to Children)

Then, two years later in 1877, representatives from twenty-seven different child and animal protection organizations from ten different states, including the NYSPCC, came together to form the American Humane Association. Since then, the American Humane Association has been dedicated to the welfare of both children and animals. Its mission reads:

The mission of the American Humane Association, as a network of individuals and organizations, is to prevent cruelty, abuse, neglect, and exploitation of children and animals and

33

to assure that their interests and well-being are fully, effectively, and humanely guaranteed by an aware and caring society.

("How American Humane Began," American Humane Association)

From 1875 to 1974—*for ninety-nine years*—various state organizations and emerging national associations educated the public about child abuse, advocated for increased legislation to protect children and rescued, housed and healed children who had been abused.

In spite of their efforts, the unofficial policy—evidenced in American homes and churches—was one of denial and indifference. Legally, in most states, parents still had total control over their children and could freely choose how to treat their kids. Many parents were loving and non-violent with their youngsters. Other parents, just repeating the "discipline" of their own childhoods, believed in severe physical punishments that would subsequently be regarded as abusive. In the 1950's, the states' child abuse laws were not consistent, well known, well understood or well enforced. Whom could children have told? Who would have believed them?

In 1958, Dr. C. Henry Kempe, a University of Colorado School of Medicine pediatrician, helped to create one of the first "Child Protection Teams" at Colorado General Hospital in Denver. In 1962, Dr. Kempe and Dr. Brandt F. Steele co-authored "The Battered Child Syndrome," an article published in the Journal of American Medical Association. This article documented that significant numbers of children are beaten and even killed by their parents or caretakers. The "battered child" description established a pattern of physical symptoms to look for and created a medical/ psychological model to follow in diagnosing cases of child abuse. "In the 1980's this publication was cited by the American Medical Association as one of the 60 most important contributions of American medicine in the 20th Century." ("C. Henry Kempe," Who Named It?)

FEDERAL CHILD ABUSE PREVENTION AND TREATMENT ACT OF 1974

In 1974 Congress passed the Child Abuse Prevention and Treatment Act (P.L. 93-247), allocating federal funds for child abuse prevention and treatment programs with an emphasis on community-based services. C.A.P.T.A. has been amended several times since then, most recently amended and reauthorized on June 25, 2003 by the Keeping Children and Families Safe Act of 2003 (P.L. 108-36). ("About the Federal Child Abuse Prevention and Treatment Act," National Clearinghouse on Child Abuse and Neglect Information) In order to receive federal monies, each state has to have mandatory reporting procedures. Most states require that physicians, ministers, law-enforcement personnel, dentists, dental hygienists, nurses, veterinarians, daycare providers, school teachers, counselors and mental health professionals report all cases of suspected abuse.

This federal act defines child abuse and neglect as, "at a minimum: any recent act or failure to act on the part of a parent or caretaker, which results in death, serious physical or emotional harm, sexual abuse, or exploitation, or an act or failure to act which presents an imminent risk of serious harm." These minimum standards must be incorporated into each state's child maltreatment statutes. ("Definitions of Child Abuse and Neglect," State Statutes Series 2005, National Clearinghouse on Child Abuse and Neglect Information)

Each state develops its own definitions of child abuse and neglect. Usually they address four main areas of maltreatment: *neglect, physical abuse, emotional abuse and sexual abuse.* Some states identify an additional category of sexual exploitation; others include that as part of sexual abuse. Some states create a separate category of psychological abuse; others include that as part of emotional abuse. ("What is Child Abuse and Neglect?" National Clearinghouse on Child Abuse and Neglect Information)

DEFINITIONS OF ABUSE:

Child Neglect: failing to provide for a child's basic physical, medical, educational and/or emotional needs. Neglect often does not feel like abuse. It feels like poverty. The mother who does not provide food, shelter or appropriate clothing for her children might seem reprehensible to us. But many times parents simply don't have the money to purchase items they need or they lack information about how to get free food or they lack transportation to even get to the food bank.

A few years ago I worked with a student whose family was struggling financially. The boy was upset because his schoolbooks and papers got wet during a Labor Day weekend rainstorm. It wasn't his fault. His family of two adults and three kids was living in a tent at a nearby campground. When I recalled how it had stormed all the previous night—poured down rain with lightning and thunder—my heart broke for him. Fortunately, we have an emergency family-shelter program in my community. I was able to quickly connect them so they could get into clean, safe temporary housing until his mom got another job and they were able to get back on their feet. His mom loved him very much. The children in that family suffered from what I would call "benign neglect." He wasn't so much abused as simply homeless.

Other examples of neglect can also be related to poverty. Children miss school to care for their younger siblings because parents can't afford childcare; kids don't get eyeglasses, or immunizations or dental exams because parents lack insurance, money, or information about free clinics. Children's health needs go unmet because parents lack the knowledge and skills to access low-cost services. Many times all that these families need is a caring advocate to give them information and help them to contact the appropriate agencies. School personnel are often the vital connection between hurting families and lifesaving community resources.

Mental-health and social services budgets have been cut significantly in recent years. This makes it even more difficult for parents to meet their own adult needs, let alone the emotional-psychological needs of their children. When parents are struggling with depression, anxiety, domestic-violence victimization, alcoholism and other drug addictions or mental illness, they often neglect their children. Whenever I reported cases of "neglect only" to Social Services, the goal was always to get meaningful assistance for the stressed and overwhelmed parents and children, not necessarily to remove the children from their homes.

Working with middle school and high school students, I called in few cases of "neglect only." Most of the time, sadly, it was other—intentional and cruel—forms of child abuse that I had to report.

Physical Abuse: physical injury to a child ranging from minor bruises to severe fractures or even death as the result of beating, hitting (with a hand, stick, belt or other object), punching, biting, kicking, shaking, throwing, stabbing, choking, burning or otherwise harming a child. Whether or not the perpetrator intended to hurt the child is irrelevant. Any of these injuries constitutes physical child abuse. ("What is Child Abuse and Neglect?" National Clearinghouse on Child Abuse and Neglect Information)

Physical abuse is probably the most easily identifiable. Bruise size and coloration can determine how old the injury is and sometimes whether it was caused by an adult or another child. Many times the physical evidence of welts, bruises, cuts, "black eyes" (and the faded scars from previous incidents) will clearly demonstrate that children have been mistreated.

Contrary to popularized misconceptions, Social Services caseworkers do not routinely recommend removing kids from their homes just because the children get "spanked." A number of factors must be considered: the kids' ages and sizes, the frequency and severity of the "spankings," what is used to hit the kids, when and how the spankings are administered and the impact on the children.

For example, it might be fine to swat a two-year-old toddler on her diapered butt for running into the street. (As a mom, I did that!) It is done for safety reasons with an explanation, "No! You do NOT go into the street." In contrast, leaving belt buckle bruises on a nine-year-old child's legs twice a week is abusive. It doesn't matter whether he didn't finish his homework or talked back to his mom or whatever. The bruises show that the punishment was excessive and abusive—not a "spanking" but a beating.

Some forms of physical abuse are more bizarre. I once had a sixth grade boy divulge that his mother poured jalapeno hot sauce down his throat the night before. Her adult male friend pinned the boy's arms behind him and plugged the boy's nose while his mother administered the "punishment." His crime? He had simply verbalized his wish that they were back living as a family with his stepfather again.

Teenagers are also at risk. Over the years, I worked with numerous adolescents who underwent every imaginable form of physical abuse. Their perpetrators were usually their parents or stepparents. Mothers or stepmothers, acting alone were the most common physical abusers. Next came mothers or stepmothers acting in conjunction with fathers or stepfathers or live-in boyfriends. More recently, I reported perpetrators who were the older siblings of the victims. A high school sophomore can do a lot of harm to his scrawny eleven-year old brother when they are home alone after school.

I reported a mother who beat her fourteen-year-old daughter with a belt, slapped her across the face so hard it caused a bloody nose and pushed her against the wall while the girl begged her mother to stop. What was the daughter's crime? She had forgotten to return a pair of jeans to her cousin. Her sixteen-year-old sister usually received just threats. Their mother woke her up early one school day morning, shaking her and telling her, "You don't smile enough. You have a bad attitude. You'd better come home from school in a better mood today or I'm going to beat the shit out of you." In their mother's opinion, the children never did anything right.

The girls' motivation in coming to me was not to complain about their own maltreatment, but to try to save their stepbrothers and stepsister from their mother's wrath. They were used to it, but they were afraid for the little ones—their new four-, six- and nine-year-old stepsiblings. "We'd like to get some counseling, too," they added, hesitantly. "You see, our first stepdad, well, he raped both of us back when we were just little. We asked our Mom to get us help but she just said it happened to her when she was fifteen and she got over it on her own so we can, too."

Emotional Abuse: the definitions of emotional abuse vary among the different states and territories. These definitions typically include behavior that is harmful to a child's emotional development; 'injury to the psychological capacity or emotional stability of the child as evidenced by an observable or substantial change in behavior, emotional response, or cognition' or as evidenced by 'anxiety, depression, withdrawal, or aggressive behavior.'" Two main components of the definition are: 1) that the maltreatment is "identifiable" and 2) that it causes or threatens to cause "substantial impairment" of the child's psychological functioning. ("Definitions of Child Abuse and Neglect," State Statutes Series 2005, National Clearinghouse on Child Abuse and Neglect Information)

How can this type of abuse be proven? These descriptors imply that we knew the child's previous level of functioning and that the parent's sudden emotionally abusive actions caused major changes in the child's behavior. That may be true in the cases where a parent suddenly behaved differently due to his or her acute medical condition such as a brain tumor. However, many emotionally abusive parents have been telling their kids to "Drop dead" or "Go f_ _k yourself!" for years. How do we show "changes" in kids' emotional responses if they have been abused since infancy? How do we demonstrate the damage that emotional abuse does to the child's self-concept over time?

Whenever I reported "just" emotional abuse I knew ahead of time that Social Services might well not be able to get involved. There is a legal threshold—a sort of "Litmus test"—that has to be met in order for them to intervene. It is difficult to prove the "cause and effect relationship" between the abuser's emotional maltreatment of the child and the child's behavioral responses. I could submit statements that the student had made to me about what their perpetrator said and how it made them feel and I could show the student's responses and scores on a depression survey, but it is so hard to quantify the impact of emotional abuse on a child.

The goal is to get help for the child, whether by Social Services mandating parenting education and family counseling or through some other alternative. Sometimes other approaches such as encouraging parents to attend free group parenting seminars—"Learn New Ways to Discipline Your Kids" and "How to talk to your Teen"—were successful and viewed as less threatening. Sometimes I involved the family's pastor or priest or extended family of aunts and grandparents. Other times, if they were agreeable, it was beneficial to find mental health services for the parents so that they could better handle the daily challenges and stress of parenting.

But much of the time, emotionally abusive parents are similar to my own mother. They have no intention of changing. They are not going to take any classes. They do not want anyone butting into their business; they think that they are doing just fine.

For all kids, but especially for children who are emotionally-psychologically abused, school can be literally life saving. We must do everything possible to make all schools caring, safe places where children receive nurturing, support and guidance—where there are logical consequences for appropriate and inappropriate behavior and where the adults are emotionally healthy and genuinely glad to spend time with them each day.

Sadly, we can observe emotional abuse occurring during almost any trip to our local grocery stores. As I walk down the aisles I hear and see parents interacting with their children. "Damn it! I told you, already, you're not getting that so just shut up! You drive me crazy." "You are so much trouble. That's it, I'm never bringing you to the grocery store again!" "God, look what you've done now! Put that back! What's the matter with you?" "I can't stand this. You just wait 'til I get you home!" "You touch that again and I'll knock it out of your hand, you little shit." The angry facial expressions, the hissing, the whispers and threats remind me of my own childhood admonishments. If this is how they talk to their kids in a public place, what are the parents saying and doing at home? Sometimes it was almost too much for me and I had to leave the store before having purchased everything on my grocery list.

A while ago I developed a strategy that makes my shopping trips more pleasurable. Instead of listening to parents yelling and threatening their kids, I focus on the parents I run across who are actually interacting in positive ways with their children. And I speak up. For example, I'll go up to a father who is gently explaining something to his three-year old and say, "I just have to tell you what a joy it is to see a dad being patient and kind with his child. What a lucky little girl!" Or I comment when I see kids being helpful, whether their parents are being complimentary or critical. "What a wonderful helper you have there," I'll say to the mother, smiling at the little boy. "He sure tries hard to please you."

Sometimes I'll try to defuse a tense interaction between parent and children by empathizing with the parent. "Boy, it can be a challenge trying to grocery shop with kids along, huh? I remember it well," I say, smiling and looking the mom in the eye. "But you've got two smart, high energy youngsters there! You must be a very proud mom." I don't know if it does any good, but it breaks the tension that was building. Maybe she will look at her kids in a different, more positive way. I don't know. Maybe not. But those kids just heard an adult give them a positive message about who they are and I come home feeling better than if I had kept silent and let negativity reign.

Sexual Abuse: includes all the following behaviors:

the employment, use, persuasion, inducement, enticement, or coercion of any child to engage in, or assist any other person to engage in, any sexually explicit conduct or simulation of such conduct for the purpose of producing a visual depiction of such conduct; or the rape, and in cases of caretaker or interfamilial relationships, statutory rape, molestation, prostitution, or other form of sexual exploitation of children, or incest with children.

("Definitions of Child Abuse and Neglect," State Statutes Series 2005, National Clearinghouse on Child Abuse and Neglect Information)

The "Fact Sheet: Sexual Abuse of Children," explains the law using specific, concrete language: "Sexual abuse of a child is inappropriately exposing or subjecting the child to sexual contact, activity, or behavior. Sexual abuse includes oral, anal, genital, buttock, and breast contact. It also includes the use of objects for vaginal or anal penetration, fondling, or sexual stimulation. This sexual activity may be with a boy or a girl and is done for the benefit of the offender. In addition, exploitation of a child for pornographic purposes, making a child available to others as a child prostitute, and stimulating a child with inappropriate solicitation, exhibitionism, and erotic material are also forms of sexual abuse." ("Fact Sheet: Sexual Abuse of Children," Prevent Child Abuse America)

It is not easy for us to acknowledge that adults harm children in sexual ways—that it happens every day in our country. Because of embarrassment, guilt and shame, years often pass before victims are able to even acknowledge, let alone talk about, what happened to them during their childhoods. Sexual abuse is the most under-reported type of child maltreatment and yet may do the greatest long-term harm.

When adults think about sexual abuse often they only think of the most severe form—sexual intercourse—vaginal or anal penetration. Yet touching a child inappropriately or making a child touch an adult's sexual organs can be just as harmful to the child. Forcing a child to give or to receive oral sex can be just as traumatic as intercourse, especially when the perpetrator is a trusted family member.

There are many types of non-touching sexual behaviors that are abusive to children as well. These covert behaviors are often puzzling and impossible for a young child to describe to someone else. Some examples include:

- Exhibitionism, such as an adult deliberately exposing his or her naked body, including sex organs, to the child

- Masturbating in front of the child
- Intentionally showing pornography to the child
- Taking an inappropriate interest in the child's physical/sexual development; pre-occupation with child's bodily functions; cleansing rituals
- Voyeurism, such as an adult intentionally entering the room during the child's toileting, bathing or dressing activities
- Engaging in inappropriate conversations about sexuality with a child: making crude comments; providing private and graphic sexual information

("Definitions of Child Abuse and Neglect," State Statutes Series 2005, National Clearinghouse on Child Abuse and Neglect Information)

Someone the child knows and trusts perpetrates the majority of the sexual abuse of children. ("Child Maltreatment 2003 Report," NCANDS, U.S. Department of Health and Human Services Children's Bureau) People in "positions of trust," such as teachers, scout leaders, church youth workers, coaches, and priests or ministers or rabbis have easy access to children, but so do friendly neighbors and parents' good friends and a multitude of relatives, such as uncles and grandpas and aunts and grandmothers. I have worked both types of cases—some in which the perpetrator was outside the immediate family and others where the molester was within the nuclear family. From my experience, the closer the individual was to the perpetrator, the more destructive the abusive experience was for my students. When attacked by a stranger, children are more likely to report it and to do so quickly. If the abuser is a respected coach or a trusted music teacher, telling what they did is not easy. Reporting your own father or brother or aunt is overwhelmingly difficult.

And mothers? In twenty-five years of counseling students, I never had a single student disclose to me that their mother was their sexual abuse perpetrator. It was hard enough for kids to report that their moms were the ones beating them or cursing them out. Those abusive behaviors were extremely shameful and embarrassing for the children. Because it was their *mothers*, they thought it must be their faults that they were being physically and emotionally abused. "Mothers just wouldn't act that way if their kids were normal kids," one boy told me. "I must be so bad that I made her go crazy."

Sexual abuse occurs in all types of families at all socio-economic levels and among communities with diverse ethnic backgrounds, racial and cultural differences and varied religious affiliations. As a school counselor, I had students from families that attended churches every Sunday divulge that they were being molested by a father or uncle or older brother. Some of these "pillars of the community" perpetrators were high functioning in other aspects of their lives and well respected in the local business world.

One teenage girl's best friends reported that she was having sex with her father on a regular basis for years. In exchange, he showered her with attention, gifts and money and even her own car. Her younger sister grew jealous and collaborated the abuse allegations.

Another family included two teenage daughters that were both being incested by their dad while their mother was pregnant with his fifth or sixth child. The sexual abuse had been going on for years but the girls said, "It's always worse when mom's pregnant. Then he doesn't want anything to do with her for months, so he comes after us even more." The girls had never told anyone because they did not think that they would be believed. Their dad was a lay leader in their church; their mom sang in the choir.

THE NATIONAL CHILD ABUSE AND NEGLECT DATA SYSTEM

NCANDS is the main source of information about children who are abused in the United States each year. The state child protective services (CPS) agencies submit annual child maltreatment statistics to the Children's Bureau of the U.S. Department of Health and Human Services. These reports usually include only the abuse caused by parents or other primary caregivers, daycare providers or other close friends and family members known to the child. Sexual assaults committed by strangers, for example, are reported to law enforcement rather than to Social Services and therefore are not included in the NCANDS report.

The NCANDS report is available on the Children's Bureau website. ("Child Maltreatment 2003 Report," NCANDS, U.S. Department of Health and Human Services Children's Bureau) It delineates the total numbers of child abuse reports made nationally and how many of those were substantiated by Social Service agencies. It identifies the types of abuse and gives detailed information about both the victims and the perpetrators.

For the 2003 NCANDS report, made available in 2005, the statistics show little change over the previous two years. Approximately 906,000 children in the United States were reported victims of abuse and neglect in 2003. Of these cases, approximately sixty percent of the children experienced neglect; nineteen percent suffered physical abuse, ten percent were abused sexually and five percent experienced emotional abuse. Seventeen percent of the children experienced some "other" form of abuse. The totals add up to over one hundred percent because some child victims have experienced more than one category of abuse. (See Chart A.)

Approximately 1,500 children died that year as the result of abuse or neglect. "The rate of victimization per 1,000 children in the national population has dropped from 13.4 children in 1990 to 12.4 children in 2003." Yet children from birth to three years old continue to have the highest victimization rates: 16.4 per 1,000 children of the same age group. Girls were slightly more likely to be victims than boys. ("Child Maltreatment 2003: Summary of Key Findings," National Clearinghouse on Child Abuse and Neglect Information)

The four different types of abuse are described separately but in reality they overlap. In fact, it is difficult to discuss "emotional abuse" as a category unto itself. The only behaviors that would fit solely into that category would be verbal abuse (name calling, yell-

45

ing, put downs, swearing, threats) or the child actually witnessing verbal-emotional domestic violence between parents.

I propose that *all sexual and physical abuse is also emotionally abusive* to the child victims. (See Chart B.) I cannot grasp how a child can be abused sexually or physically by a family member or trusted adult and not be simultaneously hurt emotionally. The emotional-psychological damage caused by broken trust and betrayal far outlasts the bruises on the arms or the bodily discomfort of being masturbated.

TYPES OF CHILD ABUSE: CHART A

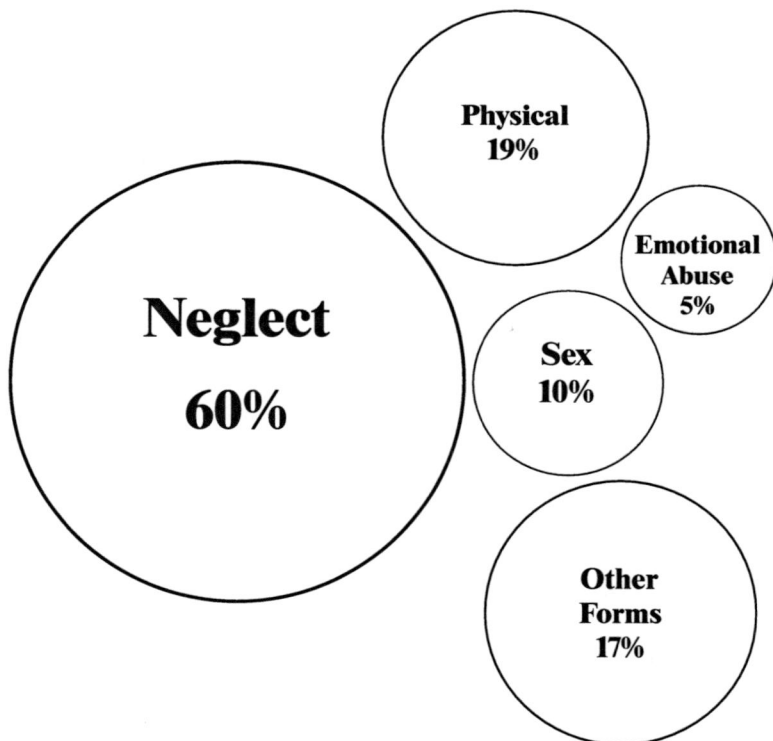

Physical 19%

Emotional Abuse 5%

Neglect 60%

Sex 10%

Other Forms 17%

National Child Abuse and Neglect Data System
Child Maltreatment 2003 Data
©C.A.P.E.R. Consulting, 2005

Types of Child Abuse: Chart B

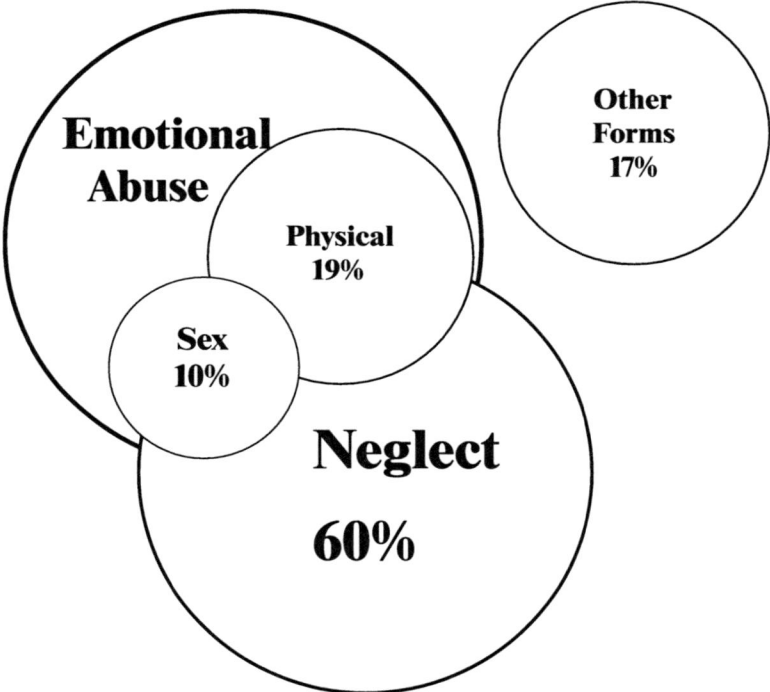

Emotional Abuse

Other Forms 17%

Physical 19%

Sex 10%

Neglect 60%

National Child Abuse and Neglect Data System
Child Maltreatment 2003 Data
©C.A.P.E.R. Consulting, 2005

WHO ARE THE PERPETRATORS?

Parents are the main perpetrators of child abuse, when we are speaking all the different types of abuse combined. (But remember, sixty percent of all reported child abuse is *neglect only*—often non-violent and due to a lack of financial resources.)

According to the NCANDS report for 2003: "More than 80 percent (83.9%) of victims were abused by at least one parent. Approximately two-fifths (40.8%) of child victims were maltreated by their mothers acting alone; another 18.8 percent were maltreated by their fathers acting alone; 16.9 percent were abused by both parents." ("Child Maltreatment 2003: Summary of Key Findings," National Clearinghouse on Child Abuse and Neglect Information) But when we examine the data for the sub-category of reported sexual abuse, parents committed less than three percent of the sexual abuse. Other relatives (siblings, aunts, uncles, grandparents) committed approximately thirty percent of the sexual abuse of child victims. Daycare providers, family friends and neighbors, and other professionals (teachers, ministers) committed the remaining highest percentages of the sexual abuse. ("Child Maltreatment 2003: Summary of Key Findings," National Clearinghouse on Child Abuse and Neglect Information)

These percentages are based on cases reported annually to social service agencies. From my professional experience, it is extremely difficult for children to report sexual abuse that is currently happening within the immediate family. Middle school girls would often disclose abuse that occurred two to five years prior to their meeting me. It often takes years for kids to tell of molestation even by a distant relative, such as the grandpa who lives in another state, let alone to tell what their own parents have done to them. More familial abuse is disclosed when the adult victims seek therapy than is ever reported by child victims at the time that it is actually occurring.

THE RESEARCH (OR LACK THEREOF) ON MATERNAL SEXUAL ABUSE

Research about the nature and frequency of maternal sexual abuse continues to be limited. Until fairly recently, it has been difficult to find statistical data about *any* female perpetrators, let alone specifically about mothers who abuse their own children.

As explained previously, the two major sources of information about child sexual abuse are government statistics (which count only those cases reported to social service agencies) and "retrospective surveys" in which adults randomly report their abusive childhood experiences and perpetrators. Based on the differences between the number of child sexual abuse victims cited in statistical reports and the higher percentages of adults who later describe how they were sexually abused as children, researchers suspect that sexual abuse, including maternal incest, is highly under-reported.

For a child to identify his or her own mother as a sexual molester is an extremely difficult task. In the case of mother-son or mother-daughter incest, the young child may well not even know at the time that their mother's behavior is inappropriate. The victims often know only that mom's behavior is unwanted and strange and makes them feel uncomfortable and embarrassed. When there is no force and often no physical pain, why would we expect a child to even consider reporting their "weird" or "yucky"experiences with mom to the authorities? It may not be until adulthood that the victim realizes that what they experienced was actually *sexual abuse.*

Other times the abusive mother will guarantee the child's silence by warning that if they should ever tell anyone, the child and any siblings will be put in foster care and/or the mom will go to jail. These non-violent threats to the well being of the family can be highly effective in protecting the perpetrator.

In addition, if "mandated reporters" such as nurses, physicians, teachers and counselors are not even aware that some mothers *do* molest their own children, many times the clues may be missed and key questions may go unasked. Mother-child sexual abuse occurs within an atmosphere of secrecy and shame. We know that cases go unreported each year.

Dr. David Finkelhor's book, *Child Sexual Abuse: New Theory and Research*, (1984), offers a chapter focusing on female perpetrators. Most child molesters are male, but some women do victimize a significant number of both girls and boys. Analyzing American Humane Association 1978 data covering more than 6,000 substantiated cases of sexual abuse, it is clear that females do sexually abuse many children. According to the study, many females abused children in collaboration with their male partners, often having lesser roles or allowing it to happen. But when female perpetrators acted alone, researchers noted "these studies indicate that female perpetrators more frequently sexually abuse girls than boys." (p.174)

In a 1994 article, "Current Information on the Scope and Nature of Child Sexual Abuse," Finkelhor summarized nineteen adult retrospective surveys conducted in the United States and Canada from 1980 to 1994. In these various surveys, adult survivors of childhood sexual abuse indicated that from seventy to ninety percent of their offenders were either family members or acquaintances.

"There is no question that women do sexually abuse children, that much of this abuse goes undetected, and that, until recently, it received little professional attention." (p.46) Then, referring to Finkelhor's and Russell's 1984 review of adult retrospective studies, he continues, "Summarizing data from several surveys, the authors concluded that about 20% of the sexual contacts that prepubescent boys have with older partners involve female partners; about 5% of prepubescent girls' sexual contacts with older partners involve female partners." (p.46)

If we apply those percentages of victimization by female perpetrators to the overall statistics for how many girls and boys experience sexual abuse before age 18:

Girls:	Boys:
Estimate 1 in every 4 to 5 girls	Estimate 1 in 10 to 20 boys
Minimum of 20% of all girls	Minimum of 5% of all boys
Out of 100 girls, 20 are abused	Out of 100 boys, 5 are abused
Of those 20 victims, 5% have a female perpetrator	Of those 5 victims, 20% have a female perpetrator
= one girl in 100 is abused by a female perpetrator	**= one boy in 100 is abused by a female perpetrator**

More females than males are sexually abused. *However, the frequency rate at which victims are perpetrated by females—one in 100—is the same for both genders.*

No specific data is available regarding frequency of mother-son or mother-daughter incest in the United States. Recent Canadian statistics are more precise, however. "The 2003 Canadian Incidence Study of Reported Child Abuse and Neglect" (CIS-2003) does identify specific perpetrators of substantiated sexual abuse. While not specifying the gender of the victims, "five percent of cases where sexual abuse was the primary substantiated maltreatment involved biological mothers as perpetrators." (Falton, B., Lajoie, J., Trocme, N., Chaze, F., MacLaurin, B., and Black, T., 2005)

One landmark research study on the subject of mother-daughter incest is *The Last Secret: Daughters Sexually Abused by Mothers*, (1997), written by Bobbie Rosencrans, social worker. She summarizes and analyzes the survey responses of ninety-three adult women who reported that their mothers had sexually abused them when they were children. The survey, conducted in 1990, consisted of a seventeen-page questionnaire composed of five hundred items with room for comments from the participants. The participants' responses give testimony to the chilling reality of mother-daughter

51

sexual abuse and to the remarkable resiliency of many survivors.

Sexual abuse statistics, however shocking, are just numbers on a page. For every case cited, there is a bewildered, hurting child who struggles to make sense out of his or her experiences.

Chapter 4

Crazy Making

STICKS AND STONES

I remember a chant from elementary school:

> "Sticks and stones
> may break my bones,
> but words will never hurt me."

They were wrong.

Physical abuse can actually be easier to take than emotional-psychological abuse. Some students have told me that they'd rather be hit with their dad's fists any time than assaulted with his angry words. I think I understand why. How a victim perceives the abuser and interprets the abuse can impact the degree of emotional damage.

With physical abuse, a youngster could think that maybe it was not intentional. Perhaps it was an accident—the parent unexpectedly "lost it." The slap, hit, or punch may have erupted from spontaneous anger. The parent "snapped," or "broke" from the stress at work or from worrying about paying the bills or from using drugs or alcohol. Maybe the father did not really mean to do it, and maybe he'd be genuinely sorry later. Maybe mom just lost her temper when she shoved her child against the kitchen wall.

A beating also leaves evidence—welts and bruises—wounds to show both the victim and the world that the child really *was* mistreated. Other people can see the marks. Bruises validate the child's experience. The child did not make it up or imagine it in the night; other people will *know* that the child is not crazy to be accusing his or her parent of doing harm. It was real. It happened. There is proof.

Physical abuse often leaves irrefutable signs: skin and bones are broken. As a result, victims of this form of child abuse have a better chance of getting help from observant professionals—like teachers or nurses. Because the injuries can often be seen on the outside, the child has some realistic hope of intervention and rescue.

INTENTIONAL CRUELTY

Children know the difference between something done accidentally and something done "on purpose." They know when they, themselves, choose to intentionally do wrong and they recognize when adults make similar choices. Children are devastated when they realize that their own parents are deliberately hurting them with their words and/or their hands.

Parental cursing, put-downs and name-calling cause emotional and psychological abuse. It isn't just the volume level of the yelling; it's the content. While hitting the child, parents spew angry and hateful words. When describing the abuse, kids often emphasize what the parent *said* over what the parent *did*. "He called me a dumb whore," the seventh grader says, crying and shaking. "Was that before or after he smacked you?" She stops to think, "I don't know. I don't remember. I just can't believe my dad called me that." The words have had a more traumatic impact on her than the physical blow.

Children know that their parents' words are *intentional* when they hear them over and over. When the mother screams, "You stupid little shit. I wish you'd never been born," night after night, it is easy to understand why her sixth grade son runs away.

When the abuse is verbal, the fact that there is no physical evidence can be psychologically devastating. No welts or bruises; no broken bones. Did he *really* say that?" the victim asks herself.

"Why would Dad do that? I must have misunderstood. I must have imagined it. Maybe all fathers talk that way. What did I do wrong to make him so mad? Should I tell someone? What would I say and who would believe me?"

Sadly, when the abuse is "only" verbal, it minimizes the chances of it being detected. All the bruises are inside, in the child's heart and soul. While the Department of Social Services can seldom take legal action in cases of "only" emotional abuse caused by parents' hurtful verbalizations, other extended family members, neighbors, teachers, school counselors and mentors can do a lot to help these children.

In cases of sexual abuse, the physical sex acts, per se, are not always the most devastating part of the abuse. This may be difficult for non-victims to understand. Often there is no physical violence. Parents who molest their own children may be very affectionate and gentle with their kids. The sexual things my mother did to me were often embarrassing and confusing but I don't remember anything ever being physically painful.

Incest victims experience the adult's *intentional sexual behavior* coupled with *little chance of rescue*. These factors combine to make the abuse so devastating. Her mother is intentionally touching her breasts but the behavior is so bizarre and inappropriate—who would believe the little girl if she dared tell?

Sexual molestation by a parent is seldom a single, impulsive act. It takes planning and calculation and happens repeatedly over time. *It happens on purpose.* The sexual moves are disguised as part of the normal hugging and cuddling behaviors of parents interacting with their children. Snuggles on the couch and tender touches in the bathtub escalate gradually over time to more and more inappropriate, overt, invasive behaviors.

Younger victims may lack the vocabulary to even describe their experiences, but they learn early on about "secrets." When abusing parents warn them not to tell anyone, children sense that the parents know that they are doing something wrong. Yet, a young child's silence is fairly easy to secure if parental threats accompany the warning.

Mother-daughter sexual abuse is the most secret taboo of all. How was I to know what was "normal" or "appropriate" behavior between mothers and daughters? I was just "Mommy's little girl," an innocent, highly obedient, only child. My mother viewed me as *her* pawn, *her* property—in some ways, a part of her. Therefore, she could say and do anything to me, and it was permissible in her mind.

She insisted, "It's for your own good" as she gave me those countless enemas. She murmured, "I love you, honey" giving me sloppy, open-mouthed kisses from her red-lacquered lips as she touched me "down there." I was always confused and sometimes frightened. It always felt weird if not just plain wrong.

Even then, I knew at least one thing for sure: my mother's sexual behavior with me was *intentional*. She had bedtime rituals and bathroom procedures that became routine over time. "We girls have our secrets," she would whisper, tossing her hair and smiling as she reached for my hand. I was not allowed to say "no" to her.

"This can't be happening," you tell yourself, as you get a little older. "I must be imagining it. I must be nuts." It can make you crazy. "She wouldn't do anything to harm me; she's my *Mother*. If she says that touching me like this is 'OK' and 'normal,' well, it must be true." All mothers must touch their daughters this way. Why else would she do this to me?

Child victims may create numerous different explanations to make sense out of their maternal abuse:

1) Mother loves me. She tells me so. And Mommies are always right and good, so this must really be OK. I must be crazy to think that my Mother would do anything bad to me. *So why would I ever tell anyone what she does to me?*

2) Mother loves me. She is always right and good, but I know this is wrong. She said not to tell anyone. It's got to be my fault. I must somehow make her do these bad things to me. *I can't ever tell anyone.*

3) Mother doesn't love me after all. But she is always right and good, so the problem has got to be me. She doesn't love

me because I'm crazy and bad and unlovable. I am the one responsible for all the bad things that she does to me. I am so ashamed. *I can't ever tell anyone.*

and

4) Mother doesn't love me. *But it's not my fault. She was the one with the problem. She used me. I had no choice. I am a good person who was forced to do all of those inappropriate sexual behaviors. It was totally my mother's responsibility; it was her fault. I **am deserving** of love and of having a happy and fulfilling life.*

Children (and older victims of childhood maternal sexual abuse) rarely arrive at interpretation number four all by themselves. They need professional help to understand the complexities of maternal incest and to grasp that it really wasn't their fault—that they are not damaged goods or bad people.

Heck, it only took me forty-something years to come to believe that.

Back in the 1950's, there would be no intervention and no rescue from a sexually abusive mother. Whom could I have told? What would I have said? Would anyone have even believed me? But why didn't I at least try to tell my father?

My father was the enforcer of mother's rules. He left no marks or bruises; he never used his fists or a belt. He just used his hands or the yardstick. The frequency and intensity of his spankings did not equate to physical abuse. The damage was psychological: fear, isolation and total obedience.

One summer my maternal grandmother visited us. I would have been between six and eight years old. (I know my age at the time based on documentation that we moved into the house in the spring of 1954 and that my grandmother died in February of 1957.) I remember that we were eating dinner outside at a round picnic table with the big green umbrella to shield us from the sun.

My mother ordered me to finish drinking all my milk. I did not want the rest of it. It had gotten warm and tasted downright gross. She said, "Let me try it." I remember watching her grimace as she took a small sip and declared, "It's just fine." I knew that she was lying.

"I think I'll just walk around while I drink it," I said, leaving the table. Boy, was I obvious! When I returned with the glass amazingly empty a few minutes later, she asked me if I had poured it on the grass.

"No," I volunteered, "On the ice plant."

"Tom," my mother said, shaking her head. "She didn't drink all her milk. Go get the yardstick." Why humiliate your little girl in front of her grandma—your own mother—for not finishing all of her milk? To show that my mother was the boss? To prove that she was in control of her kid? I thought I should be forgiven for being honest!

I ran inside the house and hid under the bed. I was sobbing. After my father dragged me out from my hiding place and just before he hit me, he told me of the "whippings" he received as a boy on the farm in North Carolina. "It never hurt me," he said. "Look how I turned out—a strong Marine! Kids need a good whipping now and then. You could see the blood running down my legs from where my daddy used the horsewhip on me but you wouldn't catch me crying and carrying on. Quit your crying. Don't be a baby! Take your punishment."

He had no clue how I felt, nor did he care. It wasn't about being hit. It was about feeling mortified and ashamed that my grandmother saw how bad a girl I was. It was about nobody standing up for me and saying that it was only milk and I had told the truth. It was about the overwhelming aloneness and despair.

My father adored my mother and trusted her blindly. When I complained about any of my mother's actions, he always took her side. When she made up things that I had supposedly said such as telling her to "shut up," he believed her and got out the yardstick. He never would have believed the sexual stuff she did to me. Or, worse yet, I thought he might well have approved of it because after all, she *was* my Mother. No rescue.

NAP TIME

My mother used me to meet her sexual needs. I do not know how early it started. But when the memories surfaced after she died, I remembered back to her "nap-time cuddling" rituals with me when I was four years old. She and I lived upstairs at my maternal grandparents' house in Oregon; my father was overseas with the Marine Corps.

Perhaps it is noteworthy that I have few memories of my grandmother even though she was very much alive that year. In the one vivid image I do have of grandma she is wearing a plaid house-dress, standing in the hallway with her vacuum cleaner and scowling at me. I remember hearing the vacuum running a lot. While I have many fun recollections of spending time with my grandpa, I can't remember a mealtime or a cookie-baking time or even a conversation with my grandmother. Not even one.

Mother and I were using two of the three upstairs bedrooms that year. There was an encased stairway in the center of the house with a regular full door that closed tightly at the bottom. I have never seen a staircase like that one in any other home. When she shut the door at the bottom, it felt like we were ascending to a whole private world upstairs, far far away from the people down below.

My mother slept in the dark "purple room" at the top of the stairs, and I was in a teeny "baby" room at the opposite end of the hallway. Her bedroom had a big double bed with a plush velvet purple bedspread and purple draperies at the windows and a big dresser with a mirror. I was in a small, twin-sized, black, metal headboard bed in a room not much larger than a modern walk-in closet. There was wallpaper in my room—a bluish-gray background with flowers—yellow and white and I think blue daisies. (Granted, my memory is helped some by having seen the room when we lived there two subsequent times.)

The third bedroom across the hall from the nursery was not used that year. It had a big double bed plus feminine pink-check wallpaper. Later, when we lived there again with grandpa (after grandma died) in fifth grade and then during the first semester of my tenth-grade year, I was allowed to have that spacious, lovely "pink room."

The "Nap times with Mommy" fondling took place from at least the age of four until I was eight or nine. That year at grandpa's house, she would take my hand and we would go upstairs together for "our nap." For this required activity, I was allowed into her bed in her big beautiful purple bedroom, and I got to snuggle close and be "loved" by my mother. I was happy. I didn't know any better. I was just four years old.

We would both be in our underwear for naptime. I would just have on underpants and she would have underpants and a bra. My mother was a full-figured woman—busty and overweight throughout most of her life, certainly for all of the years that I knew her. She was always physically intimidating to me.

I don't remember the act of getting undressed. I remember the nice soft, cold sheets and all snuggles and giggles. And she would kiss me and stroke my hair and tell me how much she loved me. She would kiss my face and my neck and down my arms. She would stroke my little girl chest and nipples and tummy with her fingertips and gently rub her fingers on the outside front of my underpants. Then she would rub a little harder.

Sometimes at bedtime she would sit on the little bed by me and touch me as she was saying "Good night." During those times, I would soon mentally check out. I focused on the wallpaper and the daisies and drifted off into my own imaginary world.

What I now recognize as dissociation, I would earlier simply call "going into the wallpaper." (I remember dental appointments during high school and choosing not to have Novocain for some procedures. I was still able to just check out mentally and go far away in my head.)

Sometimes, she did more. She'd say, "Yum, yum, yum. You're so sweet that I could just eat you up." And then she would. She would kiss me "down there," mostly with warm breaths through the outside of my underpants. But sometimes that contact evidently was not enough for her.

Those times my mother would pull my panties down. She'd rub

me repeatedly and then stick her finger up just inside my vagina "just to be sure everything is fine in there." She would make her probing of me sound medically necessary—just like the forced enemas. "Mommy just needs to be sure you're ok," she would explain, authoritatively. She would perform oral sex on me.

As the years went by, my mother developed specific routines for her abuse. She would only lie by me if I were still awake. I have no idea how many months or years it took me to learn to fake sleep. But I always clearly remembered, around age nine, my scurrying into my bedroom and pretending to have fallen asleep at nap time to avoid her touching me. For some bizarre reason, if she truly believed that I was asleep, she would quietly leave the room and not bother me. *She wanted me awake.* She wanted me to see her, to feel her and to know that she was in control. My confusion and fear must have excited her.

One of my most chilling childhood memories is of one time when I faked sleep at nap time. I was sure that she had given up and left the room. I slowly, cautiously opened my eyes only to see her standing right there by my bed! I flinched in surprise. Grinning smugly, she laughed and said, "I thought so! Gottcha!"

I don't know how frequently she molested me when I was between five and eight years. Just once a week? Every night at bed-time? Only on weekends when my father was busy with yard work and we girls had our "nap time?" I do know that I repressed most of my daily life experiences during those years. Schools, teachers, friends, Halloweens and birthdays, Christmas mornings—I recall none from that time period. I simply don't remember.

I don't think that she ever made me touch her. I remember lying on my side sometimes and she lay on her side behind me, pressed up against the backside of my body. She'd lean her arm over to touch me while she was rubbing up against me.

Throughout my childhood and even my teenage years, I was forced over and over to see my mother's naked body—in the bath-tub, while she was on the toilet, while she was getting dressed or undressed. She had huge breasts and a huge ego. "Men like these, honey," she would say, lifting her breasts up and flaunting them to me. "Some day maybe you'll have big breasts like mine and then maybe the men will like you, too."

Mother appeared to derive her pleasure from my discomfort and my embarrassment; her satisfaction from performing sexual acts on my little girl body. I was sweet and well behaved and quietly compliant. I didn't stand a chance against her.

THE PINK HOUSE IN SAN DIEGO

The pink stucco house in San Diego has been important to me throughout my adult life. It symbolizes where we lived when I began storing everyday memories—just like "normal" people—memories that I could usually readily access later on.

The house was important to my mother for a different reason. She and my father *bought* it—they were no longer renters or living in military base housing. She was very proud of *her* house. She thought that home ownership improved her status. After all, just anybody can rent.

From written records (old report cards and letters) I know we actually moved there in April of 1954. I was six and one-half years old and finishing up first grade. The early years there are a blur.

But starting when I was nine, in fourth grade—our last year of living in San Diego—I *can* remember! Mrs. Murray was my teacher and I can picture her face and hair clearly in my mind. I remember a class trip to the San Diego Zoo and trying afterwards, in vain, to draw a picture of the aviary we had seen there. I remember learning to float on my back during swimming lessons and going on a camp-out with my Scout troop and playing dolls on the front porch with some girlfriends. Their names pop up even now—"Stephanie H." and "Leslie R." I remember a "Tiny Tears" baby doll and another doll, more sophisticated—a 1950's "Barbie" prototype. And I remember my buddy—that boy named "Charlie" who told me the truth about Santa Claus and the Easter Bunny and who played cowboys with me and who had lots of brothers and sisters. There was another boy... and we planned to kiss on the last day of school but I think we both chickened out. From fourth grade on, I have clear childhood memories.

I can visualize the floor plan of our house and picture the clunky furniture and recall our first black and white television. I can see my old bedroom (and yes, the big ugly brown bedspread). I can envision the bathroom—tub, toilet, sink, and the floor where she held me down for enemas. I remember ballet lessons and not getting to perform my little part in "The Nutcracker" because I had the flu and missed too many practices. My fourth grade cerebral scrapbook is not filled with blank pages, like all the others before it. This is exciting for me. I can remember!

I dreamed back then of having a pet—a cocker spaniel that I would name "Chip." My parents' excuse for not getting me a dog was always the same. "We are in the Marine Corps and we could have to move far away and not be able to take the dog with us. Then we would have to put it to sleep and that would be too hard on you."

That did not even make sense. *Lots* of Marine Corps families had pets. I knew some of those kids at my school. Plus, and I did not think of this back then, but we wouldn't have to kill the poor dog if we went overseas—we would just find a good home for it. Plus many times the families were not allowed to go overseas with their Marine Corps soldiers. Mother and I would have stayed in California or Oregon.

I kept asking, begging. Finally they promised me, "Someday when your father retires from the Marine Corps, you can get a dog." I naively believed them.

Truth: my mother and father did not like animals. Mother thought that a dog would make messes and might get on the furniture and would also take up some of her precious time. My father grew up on a small farm in rural North Carolina but he had no use for pets either. Animals were valued only for the work they could do on the farm or for the food they provided for the family. He often told me how as a young boy, it had been his job to both gather the eggs from the hens and to wring the other chickens' necks for cooking. "It didn't bother me at all, doing that," he'd say, proudly. "I was just doing my job to help out my Mother." As a mere boy, he had killed chickens with his bare hands. As an adult, he would frequently polish his boots and clean his gun. He was a Marine. He had served in wartime. He could kill someone.

My one allowed pet was a teeny baby turtle. (We're talking about a two-inch maximum length little guy.) I named him "Spotty." He swam around in a little plastic "turtle home" all day and mostly slept. But he was mine and I could talk to him, and I was allowed to carry him outside in my hand and to play with him on the grass.

While I was at school one day, he suddenly died. I had loved him, fed him his daily official pet store "turtle food" and taken good care of him. Why was he dead? Mother said, "I made the mistake of feeding him houseflies. I guess the pet store man was right after all—those aren't good for turtles." So, let me get this right—the pet store man had told her *not* to feed houseflies to the baby turtle and she did it anyway?

I dug a little hole and buried "Spotty" in the back yard. I said a prayer and made him a cross out of Popsicle sticks. I begged for another turtle and finally they gave in. I got "Spotty, Jr."

You probably know what's coming, right? Yep, she "forgot" and fed him flies also and in a week, he was dead, too. I dug a second turtle grave next to the first and repeated my little burial ritual. I got the message loud and clear. No more turtles.

In the spring of 1957, a local farmer hosted a community "Easter Egg Hunt." My father took me to it. Children who found eggs labeled "bunny" or "chick" or "rabbit" would get to take home one of those animals. I was thrilled when I found an Easter egg that said "chick!"

So my new pet, "Bobby, the Baby Chicken," came home in a box with us. You can imagine the look on my mother's face. I have to admit, it was really stupid to give farm animals as gifts to kids who lived in the neighboring subdivision. What the heck were we supposed to do with it? Why didn't my father refuse to take it in the first place instead of letting me fall in love with my new pet? Or why not take it back to the farmer?

"Bobby" lived on newspapers in the little laundry room off of the kitchen. He peeped endlessly unless I was holding him and petting him. I think he lasted maybe two or three days. I came home from school and mother told me that "Bobby" had just suddenly died. "I have no idea what happened," she stated but quickly added, "I did *not* feed him any houseflies."

There was no funeral this time. No grave or marker. No body. She told me that she "took care of it in the trash."

Weeks later, she confessed. "I had to kill the chicken because it was *too noisy*. It *wouldn't mind me*." I asked no questions. I could not stop picturing her hitting it in the head or choking it. The message was effectively reinforced: no more pets.

As an adult, I looked back and wondered whether or not she *really* killed it. Or had my father wrung its neck, like he had back on the farm. I think she may have just taken it back to the farmer (and lectured him about how stupid the whole idea was). But if so, why tell me—an impressionable, sensitive little girl—that she had killed it? So I would know that the same justified homicide could happen to me, too, if I was "too noisy" and I "wouldn't mind" her? Scary stuff for a little kid.

The pet story eventually ended in a highly predictable way. My father retired in 1962 and we moved from California back to Oregon. They bought a house in early 1963.

It had a fenced-in, spacious back yard with plenty of room for the patio, flowers, a grape arbor, a small garden and perhaps, a dog. Once again, now age fifteen, I dared to ask.

She had run out of excuses. With a deep sigh she just looked at me and said, "We lied. We told you that you could get one someday to shut you up. I am not having a messy animal in *my* house and that's it. I want to have a lovely home to entertain friends and show off and you're not getting a dog."

I was dumbfounded. "I knew it," I yelled. "I knew it was all a lie!" But I really didn't. I had believed them and dreamed of having my own dog now that all the obstacles had been overcome. I felt like such a fool. "How could you lie to me?" I screamed.

"That's enough, Missy," she hissed, glaring at me. I gave up, once and for all.

So, why did I only begin to "store" regular memories in fourth grade? I am fairly certain that the sexual molestation ended around the time I turned nine. Nine-year-old kids don't take naps on a regular basis. Plus I was making some friends and most nine-year-olds can't keep secrets from their best friends. I think she may have feared that I would tell someone what she did to me. But I never would have told. I knew what she could do to me if I ever did.

KNIVES, CUCUMBERS AND IVORY FLAKES

As an adult, I have always been afraid of knives. In the 1980 movie, "Dressed to Kill," with Michael Caine and Angie Dickinson, the murderer used a razor knife. I covered my eyes; I was horrified. But for years I did not recall any childhood trauma around knives. Then, after my mother died, as the other childhood memories came back to me, so did those of knives, cucumbers and ivory flakes.

Mother used kitchen knives in creepy ways. That is the only way I know to describe the impact on me as a child. She would look directly at me while she chopped the carrots, talking in rhythm with the beat of her knife. I was always afraid that she would accidentally cut off her finger.

Mother would talk to me but usually about what she called "social graces." While she sliced and diced in preparation for dinner, she would lecture me about manners and morals and good old family values. I was nine years old for Pete's sake and she was giving me advice about how to get into a good sorority in college and explaining why she wished she had "married money." She would always say, "Now, I'm not complaining, mind you. Your daddy works hard," and then she would complain.

She was chopping away enthusiastically one time, with me as her only audience. Suddenly she looked right at me and said, "You know I'll cut your tongue out, Missy, if you ever tell." (When she wanted to make a point or when she was really angry with me, she called me "Missy.") I did not need to ask "Tell about what?"

We both knew what she was talking about. To clinch the deal she added, "And your daddy wouldn't believe you anyway—he'd believe *me*." That was the only time and the only way that she ever acknowledged the abuse.

My mother had lots of crazy ideas and rules about everything, including food. "Any mushroom can kill you—the poison ones look just like the others. You won't know if you ate 'the bad kind' until you're dead. So, just never ever eat any mushrooms!"

When I was in college, my boyfriend and I were fixing dinner one evening. We were going to have steaks and a tossed salad. I started to slice a cucumber. I was faithfully following the procedure my mother had taught me over the years. He stared at me in total disbelief.

I first cut off one end and then rubbed it hard against the open end of the remaining cucumber. "What are you doing?" he asked incredulously.

"I'm getting the poison out," I answered, nonchalantly (wondering why he'd ask such a question).

"What? That doesn't make any sense."

"You cut off the end and use it to rub the poison out of the cucumber," I said, stopping for the first time to think about this bizarre procedure. Then it hit me. Mother's ritual for cutting up cucumbers was totally insane. My college-educated mother practiced this peculiar behavior all these years. Either she believed this process to be effective or it was just another mind game she played on me, waiting for the day that I would do it around someone else and be totally humiliated. It was either more proof that the woman was crazy or that she had knowingly set me up for years. I did not know which explanation I wanted to be true.

Another thing she taught me about food when I was little was that green olives were only safe if you had them in martini drinks. You see, "The alcohol kills the poison." Sometimes she would give me the olives from her drinks. Ugh! They tasted horrible, soused in liquor. Looking back, she seemed to be rather obsessed with poison—mushrooms, cucumbers, olives. I don't pretend to know what that was all about.

If her routines in the kitchen seem weird, they were nothing compared to the bathroom rituals. I had absolutely no privacy in the bathroom. When I was nine (and maybe even younger, but nine for sure) she was obsessed with my bowel movements and fixated on the need for "daily regularity." Somewhere she got the idea that every child had to perform daily on the toilet (and that it was her business).

She kept daily logs of my bowel activity (or the lack thereof). She would discuss them at the dinner table with my father present; she said that she told her friends at bridge club all about "poor Julie's constipation problem." I was mortified.

"Were you successful?" she would demand, as I came out of the bathroom. If I told her "No," she would give me an enema for not performing that day. At first I would lie and say, "Yes." But later she would demand to see the proof.

Oh, my God. First she burned me for messing my diaper when I was an infant and then she humiliated me for not being "regular" in childhood. (Is it any wonder I've had a lifelong struggle with constipation? During my freshman year of college, I was often chugging prune juice and taking laxatives. Even now, whenever I am highly stressed, my gastrointestinal system simply shuts down. It makes perfect sense.)

In the summer of 1987, at age thirty-nine, I elected to have a hysterectomy. After struggling with painful endometriosis for over a decade, this was a wise decision.

It was while I was in the hospital that I remembered those ol' "Ivory Flakes." The nurse came in on my last night to give me an enema. As she prepared me for the procedure, I fell apart—tears, overwhelming sadness, confusion and panic. It was yet another excruciating flashback.

"Ivory Flakes," I grimaced to the startled nurse. "My mother used 'Ivory Flakes.'"

The nurse was only about my same age but she sat next to me on the bed and put her arm round me, and gently rocked me from side to side. She held me this way while I wept.

"Have you ever heard of giving enemas with something called 'Ivory Flakes' soap?" I asked her.

"I don't know," she answered, softly, "Maybe so."

"I remember it clearly now," I whispered. "It felt so bad and my mother did it time after time and I don't understand why."

She didn't try to second guess my mother's reasons or offer any trite sayings about parents just trying to do their best. She simply rocked me in her arms and said, "I'm so sorry." God bless her.

I had always remembered mother's obsession with my bodily functions and the fact that I was given the enemas. What overwhelmed me that day in the hospital was my sudden vivid remembrance of exactly how it had felt to me, physically and emotionally. I was re-living the experience.

Mother used a traditional, large, red-rubber, water bottle/enema kit with long tubing and a nozzle on the end. At least she would put Vaseline on the tip of the nozzle before inserting it in me. She would mix up a solution of warm water and "Ivory Flakes," which was some mild soap-flake laundry product.

I would have to strip naked and lie face down on my stomach on a bath towel on the linoleum floor. She would insert the nozzle and then begin filling me up with the warm soapy water. The pressure and stomach cramps were awful, but she would not let me get up until she was sure it would be effective—until I felt like I would burst. Then I would get up and hurry to the toilet while she watched. Each time was as humiliating as the last gruesome experience. Several times, I remember her holding me firmly down on the floor with the weight of her foot on my back. She would not let me get up until she decided that I had endured enough. It seemed like an eternity.

I don't actually know that the enemas were administered daily. Maybe just several times per week but for years. I don't remember. It felt dirty and so shameful. Occasionally my father would come in to supervise but he usually left it up to my mother. Afterwards, in front of me, he would ask her, "So, how did she do?"

When I was an adult with young children of my own, I finally questioned my parents about the bizarre practice. At that time,

I thought (hoped) that maybe my memories were inaccurate. I expected denials. But both parents admitted that yes, they had frequently given me enemas "to solve your problem." They minimized my negative feelings saying, "Oh, it couldn't have been that bad." They tried to normalize it by saying, "That's just what we parents did in those days." Well, guess what? Over the next thirty years, I have talked about this with a number of women my age and *none* of them routinely experienced daily or weekly or even monthly enemas in childhood.

Mother never apologized. She blamed me. She said that *I* made her have to do it by my refusal to go to the bathroom. Once again she thought that I had somehow manipulated my intestinal tract on purpose just to frustrate her. It was always about her; everything that made her life difficult was, of course, my fault.

Even when the recollections are painful, I think most survivors would say that it is better to know what happened than to be plagued with weird feelings and irrational fears throughout their entire lives. In the case of some abusive childhood experiences, such as the enemas, I had always remembered what was done to me but I had buried the painful emotional hurt accompanying those procedures. For other situations, such as the hand burning, I always had the emotions of distrust or fear, but I did not know the origin of those feelings. When we can't remember the original experiences, we don't understand the unconscious logic behind our lifelong behaviors. We doubt ourselves and doubt our ability to make sense out of the world. We feel like maybe our parents were right—maybe we were the crazy ones.

Survivors of abuse do *not* want their childhood memories to be proven true. We would love for the nightmares to have been just bad dreams and not our actual realities.

As my childhood memories came back to me, I would try desperately to find evidence to refute them. I wanted my parents to deny the enemas. I wanted my father to say that my little toddler hands had never been burned. I wanted the recollections of my mother touching me to just go away.

Think about it. Children who grow up in emotionally healthy, safe families do not have nightmares about being molested by their own mothers. It doesn't occur to them. They might dream about getting into trouble with their parents or fighting with siblings, or Jedi warriors, or monsters in the ocean or terrorists from the evening news coming after them, but they *don't* imagine their mother performing oral sex on them. No such nightmare is created out of normal childhood experiences.

Over the years, like many other survivors, I made excuses for my parents. I tried to minimize their abusive behaviors. Maybe she didn't know what she was doing; maybe he didn't intend to be so cruel. I wanted to believe that they really were good people who really did love me.

The fact that I am an emotionally healthy, happy adult presented a bit of a problem, too. If I were in and out of residential treatment for chemical dependency or institutionalized for mental illness, it might be easier to believe that all of these horrific things really happened to me. Was the fact that I survived proof that the abuse couldn't have been that bad? Some people look at survivors that way. How tragic it is that anyone would believe those victims whose lives were destroyed by their abuse but doubt the resilient survivors' truth.

KILLER BEES AND OTHER SCARY THINGS

Two other bizarre childhood memories surfaced over time. I cannot prove that these incidents took place; my mother and I were the only people present each time. But based on how many other memories were subsequently validated, I think there is a good chance that these are true also.

Throughout my life, I have had an irrational fear of bees. I have never been stung, in part due to avoiding situations where bees were present—I would run like hell to escape. I imagine a bee sting to be equivalent to childbirth labor pain times about one hundred.

One summer during high school, my friend and I signed up to pick beans for money. Other kids did quite well at it and got their spending money and purchased their school clothes that way. My friend was very successful but it was disastrous for me. The bean vines had flowers and the flowers attracted bumble bees. I think I lasted two days on the job. I simply could not stay there and pick beans after hearing that buzzing sound. I spent my whole time getting away from the bees to avoid certain death.

I never understood why I was so petrified of that buzzing sound. I chalked it up to just one more thing that was irrational and weird about me.

Two decades later (still un-stung) I enrolled in a continuing education workshop that examined various treatments for phobias. Participants were asked to identify their own phobias. I said that I was deathly afraid of bees and of heights, mostly stairs and escalators—I dreaded that horrible feeling of losing one's balance and falling forward. But I didn't recall ever being stung or ever having taken a bad fall.

We participated in several paired and individual exercises designed to get each of us in touch with the source of our exaggerated fears. We were told that often phobias, which we experienced as adults, were based on something that happened during our childhoods. These techniques were created to help people access their earlier life experiences at the unconscious level.

Nothing could have prepared me for what happened next. One minute I was talking about my fear of bees and in the next instant I was reliving my alleged first experience with that dreaded buzzing sound. I felt myself on my back in a bathtub filled with water. I was little—maybe two years old. My mother was leaning over the side, bathing me. She was wearing pastel blue. She slid my face under the water and held me there. I could not get my breath. She wouldn't let me up. I was so scared. And then there came a buzzing sound and she let me up. I don't know what the sound was—a doorbell or a telephone or what—but she let me up.

Had I been extremely scared to death of bees my whole life for good reason? On a subconscious level, did I somehow associate that buzzing sound with real life-threatening danger? Did my own mother almost drown me in the bathtub? I did not want to believe it. I talked to the other participants in the room but no one else was coming up with anything remotely similar to my recalled memories of abuse. Other people remembered a long forgotten scary ride on a roller coaster or a neighbor's dog that had snarled at them. I was the only one with such a frightening recollection.

Then we addressed my second fear—falling. I was expecting to "see" myself falling off a bike as an uncoordinated little kid or losing my balance on roller skates. Once again I was horrified at the memory that surfaced.

In my mind I was suddenly back at my grandpa's house—when I was four years old. My mother and I were struggling at the top of that enclosed stairway. She was trying to pull me into her bedroom. I was wearing only underpants. I ran from her but she grabbed my wrist and pushed me and then I lost my balance and fell forward off of the top landing. Over and over I tumbled down the carpeted stairs and landed with a thump at the bottom. It was so frightening and it hurt really badly when I landed.

She came hurrying down to me and picked me up and carried me upstairs into the baby room. She kept stroking my head. She told me to be quiet as she soothingly pulled the blankets up around my shoulders. She said not to tell anyone. She said to go to sleep and she would bring me some pudding later on. I curled up and thought about my daises in my wallpaper and checked out.

For the second time that day I experienced spontaneous recall—trauma and hurt caused by my mother. Could this have really happened? Even today, I still feel the need to hold onto the sidebars of staircases and I am uneasy getting on escalators. I was stunned to think that in resisting my mother's nap time demands one afternoon, somehow she had accidentally pushed me down the stairs. (I *do* think it was an accident.) Yet this incident was easier for me to believe than some of her other behaviors. It made sense.

Once again, all of the other workshop participants had tapped into more stereotypical, common childhood memories. I was the only one in the class who had suddenly recalled explicit, abusive experiences. How and why would my mind have fabricated such specific, uncanny incidents?

How can I ever be one hundred percent certain of the veracity of these two original childhood experiences? I can't. However, these explanations make sense; the pieces again "fit" well into the complex puzzle that was my childhood. Perhaps the most frightening thought is that given what I do know for sure about my mother's emotional instability and how she sexually abused me and how my messing a diaper at eighteen months invoked her wrath, these further experiences seem both sensible and probable.

When I was young I just assumed that my family was "normal" and that my parents were similar to everyone else's mothers and fathers. Why would I have thought otherwise?

I knew that family matters were to be kept private; I knew not to blab any of our mother-daughter secrets. I certainly wasn't going to tell my friends at school about the embarrassing enemas or my mother wanting to take naps with me. I did not even tell them about my father's spankings with the yardstick. I did not want them to think badly of me plus I assumed that they must receive similar corporal punishments.

My parents had to be good people, I reasoned, because each of them steadfastly proclaimed that the other parent was just wonderful. "You're so lucky to have us for parents," they would frequently remind me.

Sometimes we went to church. I thought that my parents had a seal of approval from God because their favorite and most-frequently quoted commandment was "Honor thy Father and Mother." The Church must agree with them; my parents must be right about everything. Your elders are to be respected and obeyed. Therefore, any problems or wrongdoing were *my* fault.

My father was ninety when he died. Up until the end, he would continue to tell me, "You were always the crazy one."

Chapter 5

Mirror, Mirror on the Wall

MONEY, STATUS AND OTHER FAMILY VALUES

Whenever I share my childhood story with other people, they invariably ask "Why?" "Why would a mother—*any* mother—hurt her child that way?" "Was your mother psychotic? Violent?" "Surely, she must have been mentally ill—a crazy, non-functional 'animal' who deserved to be locked up in a mental institution!" "Why didn't somebody stop her?"

The images they typically conjure up of a deranged madwoman bear little resemblance to my mother's outward appearance. Most of the time she was coiffed, well dressed and ready to meet her public. She would not consider leaving the house if she wasn't nicely dressed, girdled, and cosmeticzed.

Even at home, if she didn't look just right she would not even answer the doorbell. Once a supposedly "best friend" dropped by unexpectedly. The uninvited guest knocked on the door, rang the doorbell and even called out my mother's name because our car was in the driveway, our radio was blaring, and she was worried that something had happened. She finally left and telephoned later to express her concern. My mother admitted, "Yes, I saw you through the window. But my hair was a mess and I didn't have any lipstick on. I really wasn't 'presentable' so I didn't answer the door." She worked hard to fashion her image. Mother valued appearances and popularity more than anything else.

My mother was the archetypal society matron wannabe. She was active in numerous civic/social organizations ranging from her old college sorority to the local Symphony Guild. The year of her death at age sixty-four, she had served as president of two--a PEO Sisterhood Chapter and a Mu Phi Sorority Patrons group. (Although I never knew what these organizations stood for or what they did, she always described both groups as "very prestigious and highly selective.")

My mother was not crazy. Well, not straightjacket crazy. To the best of my knowledge, she did not hear voices or hallucinate. She seemed normal to the outside world. Growing up, I concluded that with her apparent normalcy her weird behavior must therefore be both common and acceptable.

In Rosencrans' research with victims of mother-daughter sexual abuse, ninety percent of the survey respondents reported that their mothers "appeared normal to people outside the home." (1997, p. 60) Their mothers also blended well with others in social settings, masking their true personas.

To the outside world she successfully created the illusion of being a devoted wife and mother. During my high school years she played bridge at various acquaintances' homes every week, attended numerous club meetings and went to Methodist church services most Sundays.

But church, for my mother, had little to do with religion. Seldom would this college-educated woman ever even discuss a sermon. She attended church to show off her finery and to compare herself favorably with other women. After church she spent hours obsessing over her looks that morning and critiquing other women's outfits. She would talk at length about others' lack of fashion sense or how other wives had gained or lost too much weight or how they had dyed their hair in a futile attempt to match *her* natural color. For years I presumed all mothers were equally superficial. Because I wasn't allowed much of a social life, I had limited comparative experiences interacting with other kids' moms. (The only adult women I believed to be interesting and smart and kind-spirited were teachers at my school.)

Dinner-table conversations were never enjoyable at my house but they were particularly unpleasant on bridge day. My father and I ate in silence as she maligned the women from the afternoon card party. She was especially vicious toward slender women, women who were married to professionals, women who had large, expensive homes and women whom she perceived as being more attractive than she. That encompassed nearly everyone. She openly envied their fine jewelry, whispering to me, "I should have had jewels like those! Remember, honey, diamonds are a girl's best friend."

The hostess was always fair game—her appearance, the food she served and her furnishings, even her children's looks, popularity and achievements—all were likely to garner mother's criticism. If the hostess didn't have a college degree, how could she possibly hold her own in her husband's social circles? If her son was a top student, then he was probably a nerd who had no friends or maybe, she'd say, with a wink and a smirk, the boy preferred other boys?

She would gleefully report ugly gossip and seemed to delight in scandal and in others' misfortunes: wives whose husbands were reportedly having affairs; a woman who grew up never knowing who might be her father; a couple whose only child was in prison, a woman whose husband had lost his job. Her stories seemed designed to continually remind us how much more intelligent, more attractive and more interesting my mother was than all of those other women. Further, these stories were reminders of her martyrdom; she had given up her birthright to a lavish lifestyle out of true love for my relatively impoverished father.

ROOTS

My mother grew up in a traditional household, living with both parents and one older brother. Her father, a successful traveling salesman, was absent a lot due to his lengthy and frequent road trips.

The family had a nice two-story home, and her mother was evidently well known in the community. My mother proudly told me so. Family photos occasionally graced the society pages of the local newspaper, providing evidence of status and name recognition. (Or merely proving extreme perseverance and a telephone "hounding" of the poor society-section editor? Who knows?) Her father was an avid golfer and a founding member of the country club.

Mother often praised her own mother—saying that they were "the very best of friends." (When I was a teenager and young adult, mother would often lament that she and I did not have the same close relationship, implying that it was my fault. She bemoaned the fact that I resisted reporting out every social conversation from my school day to her because *she* used to tell *her* mother *everything*.)

Her 1937 high school yearbook listings include: Girls' League president, Pep Club, Honor Society, Drama Club and Student Council. These organizations, and their adult counterparts later in life, were extremely important to my mother. Such member-ships—in her mind, at least—elevated her social position within the school community. Just as she wanted to be known and esteemed by other women as an adult, she had ached to be popular in high school. She reported having close girlfriends but few dates. "Those silly, immature high school boys just didn't appreciate what a gem I was." She also struggled with her weight, even then.

In stark contrast to many of her classmates' warm expressions, her yearbook photo is an unsmiling picture—cold, impersonal, detached. Some photographer caught her with her guard down. It was not her usual "public persona" but a precursor of what lay ahead. I would come to know that smirk well. (See photos near chapter end.)

Sorority Girl

Mother attended the University of Oregon in her hometown, grad-uating in 1941. She was a member of the Alpha Delta Pi sorority. Two different accounts however, describe her college performance: the stories she repeatedly told my father and me vs. official univer-sity report cards discovered more recently. (Appendix B.)

Not content with her actual accomplishments, my mother felt the need to embellish her every achievement throughout her life. When confronted, she would call such discrepancies "white lies" and say they didn't matter. But they *did* matter. Even more than just creating a false history of accomplishments, they revealed her lack of integrity and honesty.

So, according to mother's version of her academic record, she had "earned all A's and B's in college." She reminded me of her excellent grades when I nearly flunked out during *my* freshman year. In lieu of any understanding or support from her, I received only huge doses of guilt and shame. It wasn't until two of her old college report cards surfaced just a few years ago, that I discovered she had totally misrepresented her academic record. In fact, she earned one D, six C's, six B's and one A, albeit in "Old Fashioned American Dance," for the fourteen courses reported. This computes to a 2.0625 grade point average for the Fall quarter and a 2.5625 grade point average for the subsequent Winter quarter. Not exactly "all A's and B's."

This pattern of exaggeration and distortion might not matter to most people, but it became significant as I examined her personality and how it influenced our whole relationship. She felt *entitled* to present any version of reality she chose. Tales of her popularity with girls in high school and with both guys and gals in college went unchallenged. She was never held accountable for the veracity of her stories—about her single life in the military or why she married my father or even how she treated me. She could re-write her personal history and get away with it.

This is important because lying became second nature to her. She became skilled at it. No one challenged her—certainly not my father. Whenever she reported that I had misbehaved, he would go get the yardstick. No questions asked.

And what if I had tried to tell him about the sexual abuse? He never would have believed that it happened. She looked normal. She spoke intelligently. She had her act down. No one would believe a little girl over her. I knew it and more importantly, *she* knew it.

TEACHER FOR (NOT "OF") THE YEAR

Time and again my mother had claimed, "I taught for two years before serving in the Marine Corps." When someone says that they "taught for two years," it's reasonable to presume that they held a full-time, paid, teaching position for two academic school years. Mother did not last that long.

She graduated from college in June 1941. According to subsequent military documents, she reported having had "4 $^2/_3$ years of college." The "two-thirds" included more education classes plus student teaching that she had completed during the 1941-1942 school year. So although she always claimed that she had "taught for two years," she actually only taught high school (in a paid, full-time position) for *one* school year (1942-1943) before she joined the Marine Corps in July of 1943.

She never once spoke enthusiastically about any aspect of her teaching experience. She talked only of discipline problems and large classes of 33 obnoxious, bratty students.

When she formally reported for active military duty in September 1943, she had just turned twenty-four. She did not like teaching; she did not like kids. She was not married; she was not engaged. Her vision of fame and fortune had not materialized. She sensed that perhaps "Mr. Right" was not to be found in her hometown. Maybe he was waiting for her in the military?

MOTHER WORE COMBAT BOOTS

The information I have regarding my mother's military service from 1943 to 1946 comes primarily from eighteen of her letters home to her parents. My grandmother had saved some, and my mother retrieved them after my grandmother's death. After my mother died, I found them in a box in the basement of my father's house. I actually took the letters home with me so my father would never find them; he'd have been hurt by their contents. They revealed too much about who my mother really was.

Enlisting in the United States Marine Corps Women's Reserves was viewed as noble and patriotic in 1943. Women who took the desk jobs would free up the men for combat duty. Mother's black and white photo (professionally taken, 3 ¾ inches by 5 ¾ inches) appeared in the society pages in August 1943 before she left for basic training.

Her true reasons for enlisting had little to do with being noble and less with being patriotic. She sought the prestige of being an "officer" in the military. She would be in charge; she would have other people, mostly women, working under her command. Finally, everyone would recognize her superior intelligence and true worth.

In an unpublished article she authored in the 1970's, about being a 2nd Lieutenant in the Marine Corps, she wrote:

> We put gold bars on our green shoulder boards and added the smaller gold bars for all our shirt collars, part of our winter uniforms. Being totally honest it wasn't necessarily the need for more responsibility that I wanted to become an officer—it was just a challenge I couldn't pass up. Too, I admired the officers' uniforms and I had always been interested in clothes. The summer seersuckers were the same as the enlisted, but officers had lightweight white wool twill for dress. It was cut on the same lines as our winters—A-line skirt, a 3-button jacket but with no collar, and an open neck white blouse. The buttons were gold and gold and silver insignia, instead of the enlisted dark brown globe and anchor.

Status, responsibility, power, control *and*, it seems, some very cool uniforms! Who could ask for anything more? Well, a high-ranking, good-looking, wealthy husband would be nice.

Her military assignments consisted of working in the "WR" (Women Reserves) military uniforms offices, first in Washington, D.C., then Philadelphia, then Camp LeJeune, North Carolina. She wrote to her parents about frequent dinners and parties at the Officer's Club and of being pursued by multiple suitors.

When I was growing up, she always told me how the Marines were impressed with her "Bette Davis eyes" and her long flow-ing blonde hair. When bragging to me about becoming a 2nd Lieutenant, she somehow forgot to mention her physical problems. In that unpublished article she later wrote:

I had to have a waiver on my eye correction, flat feet and overweight. Finally the waivers arrived and we were 2 weeks late in making our debut at the "Oclub" but a short, handsome Lt. (of romantic French background) was waiting for me.

In addition to the letters, after her death I also found (and still have) my mother's old self-made "boyfriend book." She had cut and hole-punched plain front and back covers from pieces of cardboard; then cut and hole-punched sheets of paper to fit inside, tying it all together with a red ribbon. The first entry is for a "Homecoming Dance 1941." She would have been twenty-two and a new college grad when she initially fashioned her primitive boyfriend ledger. She added to it during her first years in the military. Across the page she created columns: "Name," "Where From," "Where Met" and "Remarks." Then she filled in the details about each man.

Here are some examples: "Bob B.; Cincinnati, Ohio; Blind date, just back from overseas; looks like 'Sinatra' type, short, poor complexion, but cute." Under "Remarks," she wrote "Money, good dancer. Loved my hair & hands. Expensive dates."

Another entry had just the last name, then "from Illinois, worked in office. Met again at Quartermaster picnic. Got jealous of lots of attention and date asking, Rode home on bus. About 25. Nice but ignorant. Called here but I was out."

A third description: "Joe G.; Chicago; Doubledated; Nice! Older & I seemed to impress him! Not a lot to him!! Future date refused."

One more: Irvin Mc.; Iowa; blind date, Had fun & home early. Remarks: "Got along good!! Handsome, small college, called at office but I was gone; I impressed him."

The "boyfriend book" comprised eleven pages with sixty-two different names. Some listings did not even include a last name. Some did not have a first or a last name—just a question mark and they "met on bus" or in "lingerie dept. during Xmas shopping." Whom was this chart for? Who did she think would ever read it? And why would she keep it? Her vanity and sense of entitlement leap off the pages. Interestingly, my father wasn't even in the book but she did not meet him until 1945. Perhaps the book included only her first year in the Marine Corps—1943-1944? Some of the names had stars by them. I wondered just what those stars meant.

When I was a teenager and an adult, I often observed my mother writing in a small three-ring notebook she carried with her. The black-covered notebook was always on the kitchen counter or in her purse. Leafing through it after she died, I was shocked to find a page where she had listed the names of boys whom *I* had dated in high school and college. Some of the guys on my page had coded symbols before or after their names, too. Like the stars in her chart, I wondered what those symbols meant.

LETTERS HOME

I still have some of those letters mother wrote to her parents in 1945 and 1946. Her writing reveals an immature, self-absorbed, narcissistic young woman who believed that she deserved the very best in life. To her, "the best" meant a handsome, college-educated man with position and money, the proper prominent family background, graces and social status who would marry and worship her. When she didn't find him in her hometown, she joined the Marines. When she didn't immediately find him in the Marine Corps, she continued to fantasize about the next new man on the horizon or the guys who had asked her out once or twice and who were now engaged to other women. Surely, those fellows would come to their senses, break off their engagements and come back to her (on bended knee and offering enormous diamond engagement rings).

November of 1945: She wrote home expressing her frustration. "I haven't found a husband yet!" She said, "No teaching ever again—only last resort!" She said that she had just met Tom (my father) and he was "very nice" and "has a 1942 Ford and has a accent like Boyer!" Then she switched subjects and wrote about going out with her female friends: "...we all went out to the Club for dinner—looks galore—and I met and talked to Comdr. Jones* a Navy doctor—bachelor—the catch of the Base they say! I've been trying to talk to him for weeks...About 42, looks 38 but oh, oh! Really a thrill as I am the only woman he's even been nice to! Never dances but he has with me!"

January, 1946: She wrote, "Am really getting fond of Tom... so easy going and seems to be in love with me!" "He'd make a grand husband—and a steady income!" Yet, in the same letter she was "thrilled" at the prospect of a former boyfriend (now engaged to another woman) potentially coming home from the war soon. In another January letter she wrote of her job winding down and being out of the service by July but "everything depends on the romances." She was dating my father (and would end up marrying him in September) but also still writing to two other men.

Feb. 7, 1946: She wrote home about my father: "Just a note to tell you everything is off! Yes, I mean everything!... I received a letter today from him & I see where it is all for the best! He's realized all along that I was too good for him! So we'll just be friends." She expressed frustration over five other men whom she had not seen or heard from and then praised the one other man who did continue to write her. "So I feel footloose and fancy free! Out for a good one now—rank, education and background!"

April, 1946: She wrote, "There is nothing here I want to date so I guess it is time I'm coming home. The glamour of peace time service isn't what it used to be!!" In the same letter she wrote, "Maybe a wedding out this way! It is spring, you know." (*And who would the groom be, I wonder?*) My father had been transferred a few hours away and she had not seen him for two months. Her letters imply that she had decided she was going to marry *someone*—anyone—to avoid going home "an old maid" and God forbid, having to teach school again.

May, 1946: Her discharge was imminent. She wrote that she

---

*   Real person; fictionalized name

was "fond of Tom" but in the next sentence she was excited to see the officer who had been overseas. She referred to *him* as "No. 1." This other fellow had sent her a telegram asking her to meet him in New York City. She had plans to see him the next weekend to "see how it works out." Her future depended on the two men and which one appeared to be the better deal (or who proposed first). She actually asked her parents, "Where are you planning on spending your 2 weeks vacation this year, honeys? I would love to be able to be with you till fall! Have my job or marriage wait till then. But fate will guide that I'm sure." She added, "I'll be shipping home clothes that I'll need at the beach and at home...please open boxes and have dresses cleaned if necessary & all ready for me!"

I don't know what happened during the weekend with the other guy, but I do know she returned without an engagement ring. He was not a sure thing; my father was.

Holding her letters in my hands sixty years later, her words are still disconcerting. "Out for *a good one* now," she declared, as though shopping for a car or a refrigerator. "There is *nothing* here I want to date." She wrote "nothing," not "nobody." Perhaps, unwittingly, she objectified men, including my father. They were just *things* to her—not people with feelings and needs and unique personalities and rights of their own—but objects to be manipulated and possessed. They did not matter; it was always about her. The true narcissist, she never loved anyone but herself.

Her letters exposed her true nature. The knowledge that this cold, egocentric woman would become a mother—*my* mother—the following year still gives me chills. I never had much of a chance.

THOSE SHINY MEDALS

Sometime in the 1970's my mother purchased a large picture frame with dark "velvet" backing and adjustable dividers. She divided the photo space into two sections. The left side was my father's. It bore a nameplate at the bottom, engraved with his name, military rank, and his dates of service (totaling twenty-nine years). For her right side, she had a nameplate with her name, rank and her dates of service (three years). This modified shadow box, described as "displaying our military medals and awards," was mounted on a wall in the hallway of their home and later graced a wall in my father's assisted living apartment.

Why is this relevant? Because it always puzzled me how her collection of military awards could be similar in number to my father's. Based on their comparative years of service, it defied all logic. I asked her about it once, as I attempted to study the recessed medals through the glass. "How can you have as many awards as Daddy when you only served a few years?" "Well, I *was* a 2nd Lieutenant when I got out. You know, I had a college degree when I went in, so of course, I earned a lot of awards." I nodded as if I understood.

After my father died in 2002, I was curious to know the truth. I took apart the framed award box and examined the actual medals.

My father's side was filled with a variety of his United States Marine Corps medals and pins. He had been a 29-year career Marine (CWO) and had proudly served in World War II and the Korean War. From his barracks, he had witnessed the attack on Pearl Harbor. He had survived the fires of a military plane crash with a subsequent lengthy hospital stay in Honolulu for therapy for his burns.

Problem: Mother really did not have enough legitimate military medals or awards to fill her section. She only had served three years, stateside, working in supplies and ordering uniforms, counting uniforms for inventory, signing off on inventory papers. I researched the awards and found out she was eligible for only two military medals:

1) the "World War II Victory Medal," awarded to all members of the Armed Forces who served on active duty in World War II, any time between December 7, 1941 and December 31, 1946. (www.history.navy.mil/medals/ww2vic.htm)

2) the "American Campaign Medal," for anyone who served between 1941 and 1945. (www.gruntsmilitaryu.com/acpm. shtml)

Solution: She took one of my father's hard-earned medals and simply transferred it over to her column. On her side, she proudly displayed the bright yellow "American Defense Service Medal." Visitors to our home would not know that this medal was "awarded to all persons in the naval service who served on active duty at any time between 8 September 1939 and 7 December 1941, both dates inclusive." (www.history.navy.mil/medals/adsm.htm)

Mother wasn't even *in* the military during that time; clearly this was my father's medal. I shouldn't have been surprised. Adherence to the truth never mattered to her.

But my father still had more medals, pins and bars on his side. This was not acceptable. So, she found two more medals that resembled the military ones in both size and design. She mounted them on her side of the picture frame, under the pretext of their also being military awards. Only when I closely examined them would I discover what they really were—"Good Citizenship Awards" from the National Society Daughters of the American Revolution—given to her back when she was still in junior high or high school. I was dumbfounded at the effort she spent on this ridiculous charade.

Even more bizarre, to fill up some of the remaining vacant space on her side of the military-awards display case, she added various other pins from clubs and organizations: her International Order of Rainbow for Girls pin, a high school Girls' League club pin with a cute little gavel attached by a thin chain, some other miscellaneous club membership pins, and, from out of nowhere—a Pi Lambda Phi fraternity charm. *(What?)*

My mother was competing with her own husband to have the more impressive side of the trophy case. Once again she chose to embellish the truth to make herself appear better, more accomplished, smarter and more successful than she really was. While I found her behavior to be desperate and pathetic, I am certain that my father never even noticed.

Accidental Motherhood

My parents had a small, no-frills wedding in Washington, D.C., September 1946. The woman who had envisioned a charmed life for herself, complete with material wealth, social status, travel, freedom and fun, soon found herself in small, cramped military housing on a Navy-Marine Corps base in the South. The aspiring socialite who *never* planned on having children was married only five months when she became pregnant. She was ill throughout most of her summer pregnancy and hospitalized with toxemia for several weeks just before my premature arrival in October. It was hardly a promising start for our mother-daughter relationship.

Profile of a Narcissist

As a child, I believed all of my mother's stories. She often told me that she was beautiful and all the men wanted her because she was a natural blonde with big breasts. "That's what men want. Wherever I go, men notice me. I used to walk into the Officers' Club and watch the heads just turn...It was wonderful. I could have had my pick of men to marry," she would sigh, "But your daddy was so handsome." (I believed her, of course. I did not know then that she had been so desperate to get a husband and that he was the only one who had proposed to her.)

Facts: My mother was overweight. From my earliest memories of her, she was always heavy. She gained more weight when I was in high school and college; by the time I married and moved away, she was obese. At about five feet, four inches tall she admitted, at times, to weighing well over two hundred pounds. Her self-reported dress size varied from sixteen to twenty-four, but I don't believe she was forthright about it. She was often "on a diet" and more often eating. I would observe her snacking on junk food all day, nibbling while she prepared dinner and then eating a full meal plus dessert.

She never seemed to notice the disparity between her fabricated self-image and the reality of the bathroom scales. In her mind, she epitomized desirability; in reality, well, not every man is attracted to an overweight woman, no matter how buxom she is. She would snootily criticize friends and relatives for being heavy, when, in fact, those she demeaned were often less overweight than she.

Sometimes her armor would crack, and she would break down and cry at her inability to keep the pounds off. Her tears were infrequent, however, and more often seemed contrived to elicit sympathy from my father or me.

Until college, I hadn't realized how different my mother was from other mothers. I was shocked when my friends in the dorm described their moms as "loving" and "caring" and "fun!" Even as I came to acknowledge that my mother was "weird," at the time I had little insight into the magnitude of her dysfunctional personality or the devastating incestuous foundation of our relationship.

In January of 1988, over four years after her death, I attended a one-day course for school counselors entitled "Personality Disorders," where the presenter discussed a variety of different psychological disorders. I was introduced to the DSM-III (*Diagnostic and Statistical Manual of Mental Disorders, 3rd ed.*) 1980 criteria for a diagnosis of "Narcissistic Personality Disorder." (American Psychiatric Association, Appendix C.) Here, in clear and precise language, I identified one after another of my mother's integral belief systems and behaviors.

To most people common synonyms for narcissism include: vanity, self-absorption, egotism, selfishness, conceit and self-importance. I had heard and used each of those terms before but somehow they never quite depicted the full essence of my mother's personality. The DSM-III terminology did. It described her core modus operandi: "interpersonal exploitativeness: taking advantage of others to indulge own desires or for self-aggrandizement; disregard for the personal integrity and rights of others." (Appendix C.) I was both ashamed and jubilant. My mother sounded horrific, yet I finally had a label and descriptors for her mental disorder. My perceptions were validated. There *had* been something very wrong with her; *I* wasn't the crazy one.

I am amazed at how precisely the revised DSM-IV "Diagnostic criteria for 301.81 Narcissistic Personality Disorder" embodies my mother's character: "A pervasive pattern of grandiosity (in fantasy or behavior), need for admiration, and lack of empathy." (*Diagnostic and Statistical Manual of Mental Disorders, 4th ed., 1994.*) Nine specific characteristics are ascribed to the disorder. Any five support a diagnosis; I believe that my mother embodied all nine. (Appendix C.)

1) a grandiose sense of self-importance; exaggerates personal achievements

   (Embellished college grades and years of teaching; military medals; her leadership in clubs and community organizations)

2) preoccupied with fantasies of unlimited success, beauty, or ideal love

   (High school leadership roles; popularity in school and the military; her "Bette Davis eyes" and blonde hair; the "boyfriend book;" expecting multiple marriage proposals)

3) believes that she is "special" and unique and can only be understood by other special or high-status people or institutions

   (Her memberships and positions in organizations she perceived of as "elite"; name-dropping; she was "too good" for my father; pride in being a college grad and a sorority girl; it was highly important to her that everyone knew they were homeowners, not renters)

4) requires excessive admiration

   (She would "turn heads" at the Officers' Club; the "boyfriend book;" constantly demanding attention and praise from family and acquaintances)

5) has a sense of entitlement

   ("Out for a good one now—rank, education and background!")

6) is interpersonally exploitative

*("There is nothing here I want to date;" her every relation-
ship was based solely on meeting her needs; she used my
father for marriage and a pay check and to avoid teaching
school; me for sex and intimacy)*

7) lacks empathy

*(Put down the women from church, bridge and clubs and
even relatives, with satisfaction—gleefully reporting gossip
and scandals and friends' misfortunes; lied to me about her
college grades and shamed me for mine)*

8) is often envious of others

*(Openly envious of others' homes, jewelry, clothing and
other possessions as well as their husbands, money, social
position and appearance)*

9) shows arrogant, haughty behaviors or attitudes

*(Criticized and ridiculed women from church and bridge
group for their appearances, their social graces and their
challenges in life; laughed at others for being overweight or
physically unattractive)*

Numbers six and seven appear to be closely linked. To use and
manipulate her child for sex, a mother must be able to objectify
her daughter as a *thing,* without feelings and without humanity. To
cross normal boundaries and to sexually exploit her own child, a
mother would have to be profoundly lacking in empathy.

Looking through old childhood snapshots, I discovered an
unnerving pattern. On the back of numerous photographs of
my mother and me, she had written, "Mother and Daughter" or
"Daughter and Mother" and then the date. This overt deperson-
alization struck me as very odd—I was nameless—an objectified
thing fulfilling a role. (See photos.) I looked through my own kids'
early photos plus pictures that friends sent me of their children.
Every single one showed the individual children's names on the
back.

My mother's senior
picture from her 1937
high school yearbook.

U.S.M.C. photo: Oh, how the men supposedly
loved her blonde hair & "Bette Davis eyes!"

Inscription on back:
"All set.
July, 1950"

Inscription on back:
"Mother & Daughter,
July, 1951"

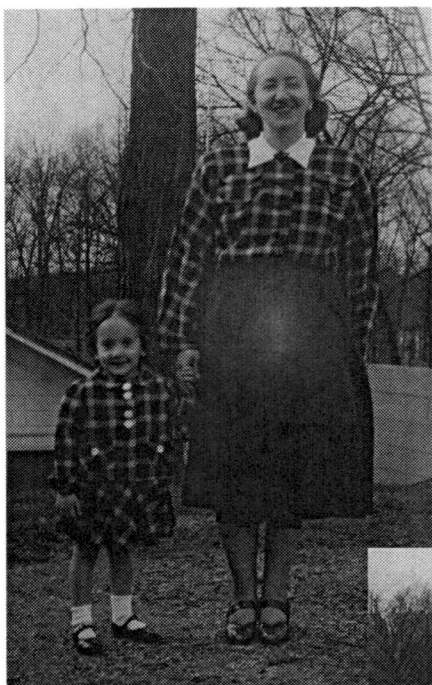

Inscription on back:
"Our twins.
March, 1951."

Inscription on back:
"March, 1951.
Daughter & Mother."

Oct. 9, 1951; two days after my 4th birthday.
Photo was taken just before my father went overseas.

Inscription on back:
"Mother & daughter
Feb, 1952"

An Untimely and Most Unusual Death

Mother died in 1983 from Creutzfeldt-Jakob Disease (CJD)—the "original" mad cow disease. The way she died of such a rare disease was as bizarre as the way she lived her life. Symptoms appeared that May: forgetting the rules for playing bridge and not remembering where she had parked her car. Dizzy spells, blurred vision, confused thinking, more memory loss and muscle spasms soon followed.

By late July she had to be hospitalized. On the way to the hospital, she was adamant that my father stop at their bank. She insisted that he go in and place her "valuable" jewelry in their safe deposit box. He said that she told him, "The nurses might steal my beautiful rings and watches. You never know—you can't trust anyone."

He told that story over and over believing that it was symptomatic of her illness. To me it sounded like a normal thing for my mother to have said and done at any point in her life. Her jewelry was prized and she trusted no one.

CJD offers a gentle, relatively quick death but it is devastating for the family. She died on August 18th. My father was inconsolable. I flew in from Colorado, met with the minister, planned her funeral and took charge of all the arrangements. During my flight, I even wrote a prayer, which was read at her service.

After the memorial service, as women came through the receiving line, they would squeeze my hand and tell me how much my mother had meant to them. And sadly, none of them would know how—at one time or another—mother had relished trashing each one of them at our dinner table.

One mourner was particularly distraught at losing "such a close friend." I would never tell her that it had been my mother who had "blackballed" her from membership in one of their women's clubs. Mother had haughtily bragged about it at the dinner table. Her reason: the woman's husband wasn't a "professional." (Never mind that my father had retired from the military and was a clerk in a hardware store at the time.)

Here was a sea of grieving faces... women who regarded my

mother as their friend. Oh, how they'd been deceived.

The room seemed filled with too many people and too many lies. I "checked out"—went on "automatic pilot." I smiled and shook hands and mumbled appropriately words of loss and thanks.

Chapter 6

Daddy

IGNORANCE, RACISM AND
OTHER FAMILY VALUES

If it took years to see through my mother's façade and to comprehend her true character, it was equally difficult for me to understand my father. Mother often bragged not just of my father's good
looks but also of his intelligence. I believe that she embellished his
attributes to further legitimize her choice of a mate. I realize now
that my father was not very bright.

But as a teenager during the '60's, I thought that my father *chose*
to play the fool. I believed he intentionally invented his illogical,
inane comments just to irritate me. How else could anyone explain
the irrational, racist tirades he repeatedly launched?

Frequently, he would offer opinions such as, "I know how to
solve these 'race relations' problems—just send all the niggers
back to Africa where they came from." Then he would laugh at his
own cleverness. My mother would feign indignation at his racist
comments, but only mildly admonish him, "Honey, now you know
that you really shouldn't say things like that."

My father haughtily asked me, "And why do they think this
Martin Luther King is so great? He's not *my* King," he would
say laughingly. "Why would anybody give him the Peace prize?
Couldn't they find an American—a white man—to give it to? It's a
bunch of crazy 'Commies' who give out those awards anyway."

In many ways my father defies description. To say he was a simple man—ignorant and easily led by my mother—ignores how opinionated and cruel he could be in his own right. To describe him as naïve and trusting suggests he was kind hearted and discounts his often-vindictive nature.

My mother *was* smart and narcissistic and cunning and manipulative; my father was easily led and naïve and trusting. He had given his full allegiance to the United States Marine Corps and to my mother. He liked being told what to do and not having to think for himself.

My father was good at following orders; he just couldn't follow very complex conversations. When he didn't understand the discussion, he would first try to change the subject. ("How about those Trailblazers? Did you see the game Saturday?") When that didn't work, he would simply withdraw or mumble sarcastic, nonsensical responses. I can't remember ever having a single two-way meaningful, respectful exchange with him.

We were polar opposites on virtually everything: racial issues and the Vietnam War especially. His car's bumper sticker proudly read, "America: Love It or Leave It." My father refused to discuss the policies or events of the war. Anyone who dared question our government's involvement in Vietnam was a "God Damn peacenik" or "commie Hippie." He mockingly made the peace symbol with his fingers while muttering, "We should line those damn antiwar folks up against a wall and shoot 'em. That would teach them."

Given the choice between listening to his racist and pro-war rantings or my mother's latest bridge club gossip, I preferred the gossip every time.

My father watched a great deal of television. His all-time favorite TV shows were "Mister Ed," a 1960's comedy show about a talking horse and "All in the Family," the popular 1970's situation comedy, which featured Carroll O'Connor as the fictional character, Archie Bunker. By the time Archie appeared on TV, I was married and living in the Midwest. But that did not keep my father from re-hashing each week's program during our mandatory, dreaded Sunday-afternoon telephone calls.

Archie Bunker was my father's champion. He quoted Archie's televised remarks to validate his own opinions. Because the show was so popular, my father presumed that everyone agreed with Archie and similarly considered him heroic. He admired Archie for expressing my father's own prejudicial, chauvinistic and racist beliefs on national television; Archie could get away with using racial epithets. Incredibly, my father never grasped that the show was satirizing Archie's bigotry. Most of the world was laughing *at* Archie, not aligning with him like my father.

In the summer of 1985, two years after mother died, I spent a few weeks alone with my father. At his request, I came from Colorado to help him clean out the basement and hold a garage sale. Only then did I fully understand his limited level of functioning. I was appalled and ashamed—I didn't know whether to laugh at the crazy things that he would say or to weep.

"Do you believe in the Holocaust?" he asked me without warning one morning during my visit. His tone was flippant and challenging. We did not get very far in that conversation before I just gave up. I would not debate his imagined global Jewish conspiracy and his attempts to re-write history. I just didn't have the energy.

He loved to surprise me with such loaded questions as I sipped my first morning cup of coffee. I never understood his agenda— were they intended just to push my buttons? Could he actually derive pleasure from such interactions? Other topics he chose for early-morning discussions included: Why the moon landing never really happened; what should be done about the homosexuals taking over our country; the evils of interracial marriage; the need for a military draft; and did I know that men who wear beards are really Communists?

If he had been a compassionate and caring person, I would have more easily accepted his cognitive limitations. Alas, he was not only slow at understanding things but also judgmental and hateful and mean spirited.

"What did you do to your hair?" he growled, when he met me at the airport that summer. "You're curling it just like a Negro's!"

Whispering then, he said, "See, I said 'Negro.' You thought I was going to say 'nigger,' huh? See, you don't know everything. Missy!" I fought the urge to turn around and get right back on the plane.

In a crowded restaurant later that day of my arrival, a waitress was loaded down with empty bowls and plates. As she passed by our table, a small salad bowl slipped off her tray into my father's lap. The bowl was lightweight. It was empty. Dropping the bowl did absolutely no harm. Still, my father became enraged. He yelled at the embarrassed waitress, "You stupid girl! Did you see what you did? You spilled that all over me!"

She apologized profusely but to no avail. "I can't believe they even hired somebody like you," he roared. "If I was your boss, I'd fire you!"

Tears welled up as she walked away, red-faced and humiliated. Other patrons stared at my father in disbelief. I was mortified. We barely spoke during the rest of our meal.

As we left the restaurant, I whispered my deepest apologizes to our waitress and slipped her the tip my father had noisily declared he would not be leaving "for such a clumsy idiot."

Driving home in his car he broke the silence by saying, "Well, I suppose you think I was too hard on that girl, huh?"

"Yes, you were," I answered. "It was just an accident and no harm was done. You had her in tears. I don't understand why."

"Well, because she could have hurt me," he rationalized. "People shouldn't be so sensitive like her and that goes for you, too."

This was not early dementia. It was nothing new. This was the same father I had grown up with during the '50's and '60's. Now that my mother was no longer around to muzzle him, he was free to malign whom he wanted whenever he wanted.

I shook my head. Why did I continue to hope that each time I visited he would be different—that he would have had an epiphany?

It was a very long two weeks.

Roots

My father was born in Gibson, North Carolina. He was one of nine children—six boys and three girls. Two died in infancy. His father worked on a farm; the kids helped in the fields when they weren't in school. He said that they were always poor and then my grandfather lost what little he did own during the Depression.

I believe the farm was located in McColl, South Carolina. I visited them only one time that I was old enough to remember.

My father graduated from nearby Gibson High School in 1930 in a class of twenty-nine students. After working odd jobs for a few years, he joined the Marine Corps in 1933. He hoped to earn a steady income and to be able to send money home to help his parents.

Other details are a bit sketchy and are loosely based on stories that he or my mother told me. Pieced together, they form a picture of my father's roots and a glimpse of the man that he would become.

He told me that his brothers and sisters sometimes played tricks on him. One year all the children received candy bars in their stockings from Santa. His brothers gave him a taste of unsweetened baking chocolate and told him it was real chocolate. After that he hated chocolate for years and always gave all his chocolate candy to his siblings, thinking it was bitter. He would laugh each time he told the story. I always thought it was sad.

At night, he would sometimes lie in bed listening to his father mount up to ride with the Ku Klux Klan. He seemed proud in recalling his father's KKK membership. When I was old enough to understand what the KKK meant, I was horrified and I asked him more about it. He was nonchalant and said that he didn't *think* his own father had ever killed anybody but he "couldn't be sure."

He spoke of receiving beatings from his father—that he must have deserved. He reasoned that if a parent severely punished a child, the child must have deserved it. The parents were *always* right.

I asked about his mother. I wanted to know what she was like.

He said, "I loved her very much." He remembered how much she had liked it when he brushed her hair. "She had hair clear down her back."

I wanted to learn more about her. He said that she was "different" from other people, explaining, "She always treated 'the colored' just like normal people. We had a Negro gal who worked for us and my mother wanted her to sit at the table and eat with us."

"What happened?" I asked.

"Well, my mother got her way. After that she ate with our family all the time."

I liked what I heard about my grandmother. I wondered why my father did not choose to model his life after her.

He told me that he had dropped out of school at the start of the eleventh grade to work on the farm and then returned to school and took his junior and senior years at the same time in order to graduate with his class. I still have his high school diploma. It is huge—perhaps two feet by three feet—a rectangle of aging parchment—proof that he did graduate from high school.

Even though he was fourth of the nine children by birth order, my father outlived all of his siblings. Cancer took his sisters, one brother died in a military plane crash, one brother committed suicide and one brother died at eighty-eight in a nursing home. My father remained devoted to his parents. They lived to be in their eighties and he continued to help them financially until their deaths.

I have photos of me with my paternal grandparents—as an infant and during the one visit back to the Carolina farm in 1957 when I was nine years old. After my mother died, I asked him why we had made only the one trip back to North Carolina. "Your mother didn't want to go," he replied matter-of-factly.

"What?" I exclaimed. "They were your *parents* and you had lots of brothers and sisters to see. I remember having fun the time we went. I helped grandma shell peas, and I fetched eggs from the chicken coop. I remember meeting all my cousins and using the outhouse and taking a bath in a big metal pan on the kitchen floor near the stove!"

"Like I said," he mumbled, "Your mother didn't want to go back. She hated the heat, and they didn't have a nice house or anything."

Over the years, my father made other trips back East but always alone. I think he eventually paid for his folks' new indoor plumbing, too.

"Well, if she didn't want to go, why didn't you just take me along? Was it because it cost too much money?" I asked.

"No, your mother didn't want you to go off with me. She said she would miss you too much."

SEMPER FI

My father joined the Marines in August of 1933. He always claimed that he had lied about his age to get into the Corps. Later I discovered that he *was* already twenty-one at the time he enlisted so lying about his age made no sense. But my father's official military papers list his birth date as June 12, 1911. His 1955 request to officially change his recorded birth date to his real birthday of June 5, 1912 gives no reason for the error.

The Marine Corps gave him an identity and a purpose. It provided security and status to a young man who had neither. In exchange he offered his total allegiance for twenty-nine years. He believed that the Marine Corps was the best branch of the military—the few, the proud—the strongest, the smartest, the best. Before and above all else, he was a Marine.

Military documents show his rank was a Private, 1st Class in 1935 and a Corporal in 1936. He re-enlisted in 1939 and again in 1946. He permanently retired as a CWO-4 in 1962. When I later asked him why he had not served just one final year—to have the distinction of serving thirty years in the Corps—he said it was because my mother wanted out of southern California. She told him she would not put up with the hot climate and the lifestyle and living in military base housing (Camp Pendleton) for even one more year. He did not challenge her. She won. She *always* won.

He never talked to me about his early military experiences. I know little of what he did in World War II or the Korean War. He *was* at Pearl Harbor on December 7, 1941 and he relished discussing that experience. (From his barracks window, he saw the bombs dropping.) Until his death at age ninety, he maintained memberships in the Retired Officers Association and the Pearl Harbor Survivors Association.

When I was a child it seemed that the Marine Corps was the most important thing in the world to my father. He polished his shoes and cleaned his gun with pride. He carried a "swagger stick." (No, he never used it on me.) He looked good in his uniforms. Sometimes he wore his "dress blues" and posed for family photos with his Marine Corps sword at his side. The effect was quite daunting. I thought that he loved the Marine Corps more than anything.

In seventh grade, I first learned of Nazi Germany. Under the covers with my flashlight, I secretly read a book about Hitler and the prison camps. It broke my heart. Later, we briefly studied the Nuremberg trials. I was dumbfounded that the war criminals would attempt to justify their behavior as "just following orders" from their superior officers. But I remember believing at the time that my own father would have done anything his superior officers told him to do.

That was one of the most frightening realizations of my childhood because second only to the Marine Corps' was my mother's authority over him. There would be no help for me from this man. "You will do what your mother tells you, young lady, and don't you ever talk back to her. She's your *Mother!*"

"Yes, sir," I'd whisper with a hopeless sigh.

WITH COMPASSION FOR NONE

When survivors of father-daughter incest disclose their victimization, they are frequently asked, "Did your mother know?" Some mothers may suspect inappropriate behavior but feel powerless to intervene for a wide range of reasons—from financial dependency on the perpetrator to fear of spousal violence to distrust in the legal system's ability to help victims. Others may unconsciously ignore the symptoms of their daughters' abuse to protect themselves from the painful memories of *their own* childhood molestation. Some may remain genuinely unaware.

In my case, I am certain my father was totally unaware that my mother was sexually abusing me. He was ignorant of the behaviors that constitute sexual abuse, and he knew nothing about stages of child development or appropriate parental interactions. He deferred all parenting decisions to my mother—whether it was required "naps" and enemas at age nine or not letting me drive a car at sixteen.

My father was stationed overseas (1951-1952) during the Korean War when my mother initiated the most explicit molestation. If my father *had* been present in the home at the time, it would not have made any difference. Sadly, he would not have intervened on my behalf. He blindly trusted my mother—never questioning her authority and oblivious to her potential for doing harm.

Mother often reminded him that *she* was college educated, cultured and more sophisticated and therefore, far more knowledgeable about everything. She was *in command* of their marriage. Mother was the boss. She controlled their finances, she organized his weekends and vacation time and she decided what furniture they would own. And, regrettably, she was also in charge of me. If this woman had deftly explained away my burned hands at eighteen months, surely she could silence questions about any other injuries that might occur over the years.

My parents shared an important character deficit. Both lacked the ability to *empathize*. He ridiculed others' emotional problems, even labeling Vietnam vets with Post Traumatic Stress Disorder as "sissies" and "babies." "You didn't see me come home from war crying and complaining! They're a bunch of wimps!"

He had no sympathy for victims of any crime. Women who were raped "deserved it for dressing like whores." People whose cars were stolen "should have locked their cars or just parked them someplace different." A man who was assaulted "must have done something to ask for it."

106

My father showed no compassion towards animals or children. Animals were to be used for work or pleasure. As an adult, I saw him kick our two kittens when their behavior annoyed him. If children misbehaved, they deserved whatever punishment their all-knowing parents doled out. Once when I was visiting, a case of extreme physical child abuse was reported on the evening news. He belittled the victims for "being weak" and "crying about nothing."

My father would have denied that he and my mother ever emotionally mistreated me because he had no concept of emotional abuse. He also had no concept of emotional health. He never discussed feelings—his or anyone else's. There was no introspection or insight. As a teenager, I was never sure whether he was incapable of higher-level thinking or had simply chosen, long ago, not to expend the effort.

PAPA'S PEARLS OF WISDOM

Most adult children can recall some of their parents' favorite expressions. Such characteristic sayings may offer wisdom and comfort long after the deceased parents have moved on. On the other hand, here is what I remember from my father:

1) "Parents should talk softly and carry a big stick." *(His version of a Theodore Roosevelt quote; except my father didn't suggest carrying the stick as a bluff or to avoid confrontation; he meant, "You don't have to raise your voice, just whack 'em one!")*

2) "We might have been poor but we always knew we were better than them niggers." *(Well, thank goodness for that!)*

3) "Children should be seen and not heard...heck, I'm not even sure *you* should be seen." *(What a loving thing to say.)*

4) "The best show they ever put on TV was 'Mister Ed!'" *(Proclaimed in 1997 while he was watching re-runs of the show.)*

5) "I am sick and tired of hearing about these poor homeless

people. Our church is always feeding them and everything. You know what I say? I say to tell the creeps to get a job like everyone else, or go back home. How dare they hang out at our church!" *(Shared with me, driving home after church services, August 1997. We had taken Communion just fifteen minutes before, and the sermon that Sunday was about reaching out to others; feeding the masses.)*

6) "Why don't you just go back to Russia, you damn Commie Hippie!" *(Yelled from the car window to a gentleman who was walking along the University of Oregon campus in the summer of 1985. Why? Because the other man sported a beard? Because he was carrying a briefcase?)*

7) "This country was great until this 'Women's Movement.' Now it's ruined. It all started when your aunt wore a pantsuit to church one Sunday." *(His idea of making conversation at the train station, Christmas, 1983.)*

During my visits in the 1980's and 1990's, he became increasingly critical of everything about me. I needed a strategy to cope with his nastiness so I decided to carry a small notepad to maintain a record of what he said. I also tallied his daily putdowns of people by categories—minorities, me, my children, women in general and relatives. It gave me a focus. Instead of being devastated by his hurtful comments, I chose to view each inane assertion as an opportunity for another tally mark. Each morning, for example, I guessed, "How many anti-Semitic comments will he make today?" Usually, at the day's end, I had estimated too low.

Some examples include:

1) *"I* try to drive defensively," he bragged to me. "You are a horrible driver. I can't believe they even let you drive in Colorado!" *(1991; I was on the Interstate, driving at the legal speed limit and keeping with the flow of traffic. He screamed that I was driving too fast. I slowed to ten miles under the limit as cars passed us. For an hour, he criticized my every maneuver. I finally pulled into a rest stop and*

asked him to drive.)

2) "You are too nice to people." (He was referring to my inter-actions with his regular yardman/handyman and a cleaning woman he had hired to help clean before selling his house. "They work for *us.* I'm paying them. You don't have to make conversation on my time and money." *(Summer, 1999; at his request, I flew out for two weeks to move my father into an assisted-living facility and to prepare his house for sale. Karl, the yardman, was a tremendous help to me with lift-ing and hauling boxes and bags of junk to the dump. He had worked for my father for over twelve years. During that time, my father had never inquired about Karl's family. He never knew or cared that Karl was married and had children.)*

3) As I settled my father into his new, assisted-living apart-ment, the lady across the hall knocked on the door. My father opened it. She had her little dog in her arms. She introduced herself and her dog and enthusiastically welcomed my father to the residence building. "I don't like dogs," he bellowed and slammed the door in her face. *(Summer, 1999)*

4) He offered me a piece of chocolate from a box of candy. I declined.

"Well, did I say anything?" he asked me.

"What?" I responded.

"Did I say anything about how fat you've gotten? Huh, did I? NO, I didn't."

(2001; I had gained a few pounds since the previous sum-mer. I was still a size ten or twelve—considerably smaller than my mother at her lightest.)

5) I had joined my father for breakfast in the assisted-living dining room when the server asked if I wanted coffee. I responded enthusiastically, "Yes, sounds great! I haven't had any yet." (I was staying with a girlfriend who happens to be

a tea drinker so I had not had any coffee that morning.)

"What? She didn't even make you any coffee?" my father exclaimed. "Some friend she is!"

"No," I said, "It's fine—she and her husband are tea drinkers."

He leaned over then, and in a low voice said, "Well she's probably afraid of turning Black!"

"What are you talking about?" I asked incredulously.

His eyes darted to the nearby tables as if to see if anyone was listening. He leaned over and whispered his secret warning, "Well, some people think you can turn Black like a nigger from drinking too much coffee!"

He sat back in his chair, appearing satisfied and smug. "You just never know," he added with a smirk. I was speechless.

For a while my father had shared his meals with another man at a small table by the windows. I joined them one morning and found the other fellow to be an interesting conversationalist. I took him aside and asked how he could stand talking with my father every day. With a wink and a smile he motioned as though he was adjusting his hearing aid. He was able to just tune out my father! Unfortunately, I had no such device.

6) No visit was ever complete without my father rebuking me for being both immoral and mentally ill. Even when twenty years and then thirty years had gone by and my son was a grown man—my father censured me yet again over how I had disgraced the family by getting pregnant in 1968. Never mind that he had already called me a "whore" back then and that he and my mother had refused to come to my wedding. My annual visits provided more opportunities to attack. Neither my graduating from college two weeks before my son was born nor my years of being a devoted wife and mother could atone for my sin. There was no point in trying

to talk with him. His job was to chastise me and mine was to sit there silently and take it. He was my father and now that my mother was gone, his word was law.

"Don't you look at me that way, Missy!" he'd snarl. "I will talk about this any time I want. I will never forgive you. You—you're the one who ruined everything."

The second topic of conversation was my sanity. Sometimes I just could not tolerate his racist remarks. When I asked him to stop, he would tell me that I was "crazy." He said that I "needed to see a psychiatrist because" I was "too nice" to everybody.

One time I dared challenge something he had said about homosexuals. I talked about how difficult it is for high-school kids to come out to their parents. Thinking he would then have some newfound compassion for their struggles, I instead found myself looking at his clenched fist and witnessing his fury. "You just love those little queers, don't you?" he yelled. "You... you need to see a doctor for your head. You have problems! I can't believe you... you even have a job." Red-faced, he shouted, "You belong in a mental hospital—that's what I think!"

I went to bed.

The next morning he acted like everything was normal. "What a nice visit we've had!" he said. "I hope you come again soon, honey."

When I was dating my current husband, I told him of my parents and my childhood. When Jeff and I married in 1994, he promised me, "You will never have to face this man alone again."

We drove up to Oregon to visit in 1995. We only stayed with my father for a few days but afterwards my husband said, "I'm sorry, honey. I don't think I can ever do that again." He found it unbearable to be around the man. Curiously, I had thought my father was on his "best behavior" around his new son-in-law.

FIVE DAYS IN AUGUST

It was summer, 1997. I had to make the annual visit to my father's house and this time I was exceptionally apprehensive about going alone.

My husband was committed to his sister's home re-modeling job near San Francisco; we had driven his truck there from Colorado. He would work there for five days while I spent time with my father in Oregon. How bad could five days be?

From August 2nd through 6th, 1997 I kept a journal with daily (sometimes hourly) entries. It was *the* most difficult time I would ever experience with my father and only the journaling and daily phone conversations with my husband kept me sane. I would have given anything for a silent, invisible witness.

Sat. 8/2/97: My arrival was met with typical, low-level criticisms: my suitcase was "too big," my permed hair was "too kinky...You know what we say about that! Why, when I was growing up nobody had kinky hair but" (pause, whisper) "those Negroes." (Giggle) "Just kidding. Ha ha."

Later we picked up a friend of his and went out for dinner. Any time we spent with friends or relatives was preferable to being alone with him. Those times my father showed amazing self-control; he *could* suppress his racist banter when we were with other people. For the most part, he would make non-offensive small talk (usually about sports) or just sit quietly. But that was crazy making for me, also. It indicated he *was* aware of what he was doing and could control it if he so chose.

Sunday, 8/3/97: We attended Methodist church services. On our way back to his house came his previously quoted tirade about the homeless. He called the minister "a bleeding heart" for "always wanting to help people." I was speechless.

Next he told about my Uncle Doug (deceased) who "just hated having 'niggers'—your uncle Doug's word for 'em, not mine—well not these days—around." He explained that Doug had lived his last years in a nursing home in the South where most of the nursing home staff were "Negroes" and how Doug had had to let them touch him. He delighted in this story. "I wouldn't have some nigger touch me," my father hissed.

Later that day, he showed me some old Carolina photos and I asked about his father—my grandpa. He said, "My dad was very strict. When we did something wrong he gave us what we deserved—a whipping—with the buggy whip. It hurt bad and your legs would bleed but we thanked him for it cause we deserved it...well, maybe not at the time but later on...You didn't see *me* crying," he declared.

He continued, "The last time he did that to me he cut my legs and I was about fourteen and I looked him in the eye and said, 'Don't you ever whip me again or I'll kill you.' He never did."

"Were you close to him?" I asked.

"Well, no, but he was my father and I respected him."

Monday, 8/4/97: The third day started with the usual remarks. I wondered if anyone else might start their morning conversation with "So, how 'bout these homos? What do you think of them, huh?"

We ran errands and ate lunch at Arby's. He was rude to the waitress. He mumbled that he wanted coffee. Not understanding him, she asked him nicely if he wanted anything to drink. He bellowed, "I just TOLD you—coffee. What's the matter with you—can't you hear?"

After our lunch, he drove downtown to point out some new buildings and businesses. At a busy intersection, he started to turn left on a red light and narrowly missed hitting a woman and two children who had started to cross in front of his car, legally, with the green "Walk" sign. I screamed. They jumped back in disbelief as he slammed on his brakes.

"Boy, that was lucky!" he exclaimed. He was relieved that his new car wasn't hit. "I can't have another accident or my insurance will go up!" He expressed no concern or remorse at having almost hit the three pedestrians.

That evening my father started talking about my husband. He said, "You're not going to call Jeff now are you? It's probably too late. Besides, let him call you. He never calls you. He should call you *if* he loves you so much."

"So, do you think Jeff is faithful to you?" he suddenly asked.

"WHAT?"

"You heard me. You never know, do you? You know what they say—the wife is the last to know."

Dumbfounded, I queried him back, "Well, were you faithful to mother?"

He said, "Well, of course, I was! But, of course, your mother was a blonde!"

"WHAT?"

"Well, I'm sure Jeff loves you but you know how it is."

"No, Daddy, how is it?" I asked.

"Well, nobody can resist a pretty face. Every guy was jealous of me with your mother...that beautiful hair...her bosom...."

I just sighed and shook my head. He turned on the television to watch the news.

Tuesday, 8/5/97: Tension had been building each day but I figured it could not get much worse. I was wrong.

I don't remember what we did Tuesday morning—the conversations began to blur. Every day he brought up something negative or judgmental about African-Americans, Jews, homosexuals, Democrats, the University of Oregon, public education, my generation and, more specifically, me.

My uncle and aunt had invited us to their Masonic Lodge picnic that afternoon. I was looking forward to spending time with them. My mother's only sibling and his wife were the opposite of my parents—loving and kind and optimistic and fun.

They picked us up in their car. My father made his usual quality of small talk. Not "How have you two been?" or questions about their children, grandchildren, health, travels or anything personal. "So," my father said, getting into their car, "What do you think about women in politics? Personally, I think we have too many women in politics."

I had a nice time at the picnic except for my father repeatedly interrupting my conversations with other people by grabbing my arm and pushing me over to meet someone else of his choosing. It was rude and bizarre.

After we returned home I tried to call my husband in California.

"I thought *he* was going to call you to-night?" father said.

"Well, he hasn't so I'm going to try him," I answered.

I tried several times and got a busy signal each time.

"Did you get him *this* time?" asked dad, sarcastically, after my third for fourth try.

"No, I got another busy signal."

"Oh, he's probably talking to his girlfriend. You never know about these guys." (He says this without any chuckle or twinkle in his eye. If this is his idea of a joke, he doesn't indicate it.) "After all, you left him to come up here."

I ignored his comment. Even so, things got worse.

We sat down around ten o'clock to have some cake. He started talking about the Masonic picnic.

"I didn't have a good time," he stated. "They're all so uppity and think they're better than everyone else."

"What?" I said, totally surprised. "What did anyone say that made you think they feel superior?"

"I don't have to answer to you!" he yelled.

"I'm just trying to understand what happened, Dad. We must have had two completely different experiences. I felt a very warm welcome, and I had a good time."

"There you go arguing again. I don't have to answer to you! I refuse to answer on the grounds that it might incriminate me. So there."

"What are you talking about?" I asked.

"You think you're so damn smart—you, you come here and challenge everything I say. Why do you do that? Why can't you just be nice?" He stomped out of the room.

It was now almost eleven o'clock. I went in the den to watch the news on TV. He returned in about ten minutes and sat down in a chair right next to me. My attempts at making neutral conversation were ignored. I left the den and went to bed.

Around eleven thirty he pounded loudly on my bedroom door. I came out into the dining-room area. He was irrational and visibly shaking with anger.

"How can you do this to me? You're my daughter," he shouted. "You're so mean...you're evil! You don't agree with anything I say—you, you think you're so perfect, Missy—you're just like your aunt and uncle...*You just love everybody, don't you?* You think you're so much better than everyone else."

He was livid. I could not even respond.

He continued, "You're killing me...You used to be so nice. . .such a sweet girl.... I don't know what happened to you. I used to like you. What the hell happened?"

"When?" I yelled back. "*When* did you ever like me? How old was I when you liked me?"

"FOUR!! You were four!!! You were such a nice little girl. What happened?" he screamed.

His irrational tirade continued. "You're crazy! You must have duped everyone at your school! How did you ever get a job? You're so evil! You need to see a crazy-people doctor. Maybe you're possessed or something."

He came at me then in the dining room. He gripped my arms to my sides, held me hard and close to him, my back against the wall. I could feel him trembling with rage as he spewed how I was "so evil." Now I was afraid. If I said anything more, he might hit me or go for his gun, which he kept loaded next to his bed. I had never seen him so frenzied and out of control.

I was immobilized with fear, scared that *anything* I said would be twisted and misconstrued. Finally he said, "You just think about this Missy! I don't know how you can stand yourself! You just go to bed and think about how awful you are!" Then he left.

I went in my bathroom and threw up. I considered calling a cab and staying at a motel that night, but that could have made things worse. I did not know what my father might do. He had my flight information for the next day; he might come to the airport and make a scene. I got little sleep that night.

Wednesday, 8/6/97: I awoke around six o'clock, took a shower and packed. At breakfast, he was cold and distant but made no

116

mention of the previous night. We made innocuous small talk as he drove me to the airport.

As in 1985, he hugged me goodbye and again said how wonderful the visit had been and how he only wished I could have stayed longer. Numb and exhausted, I boarded the plane to San Francisco.

I had bounced back fairly quickly from all my previous family visits to Oregon. This time I could not shake the hurt and the insanity.

Everything felt so normal at my sister-in-law's house. How could sane, caring people ever grasp what my family was like? Just being there felt surreal—like an episode from "The Twilight Zone."

The next morning my husband and I loaded up the truck and left for home. As soon as we were safely alone in the cab and out of site, I totally "crashed." For hours, I read my notes to him and sobbed uncontrollably. As I struggled to make sense out of my visit *and* my childhood, waves of grief and despair and shame overwhelmed me.

I had little fight left in me. Never had I experienced such exhaustion.

After we returned home I spent hours entering the notes into my computer. It was appalling to again read my father's words, verbatim.

But it was affirming also. I now had something to re-read when I was tempted to tell myself, "Oh, it couldn't have been so bad."

TAPS

My father died on August 18, 2002 at age ninety, on the exact anniversary of my mother's death nineteen years earlier. They are buried together at Willamette National Cemetery (for military veterans) in Portland, Oregon.

I held a small, nice service for him at the mortuary, complete with multiple bouquets of flowers and two eight-by-ten glossy photos of him—one in his uniform and one in a suit. I smiled a lot and checked out even more. *(Who says dissociation is a bad thing?)*

Most of his remaining possessions I gave away. His furniture went to a victim of domestic violence who, together with her young child, was starting a new life and had nothing. His clothes went to a local clothing bank. I shipped home several boxes of memorabilia, including his Marine Corps sword and *his* well-earned medals.

From time to time, I look through old photographs. They probably appear similar to those taken of other families during the 1950's and 1960's. How could anyone have known what was happening behind closed doors?

And I still have my old baby book. Under the "First Discoveries" section there is a listing for "First Words." According to the entries in my mother's handwriting, my first words were "Da,da" and "Bye, bye."

Then the book's printed script reads, "First said 'daddy'" and she had written "July & August '48."

The next line of the book's printed script reads, "First said 'mamma.'" That entry space remained forever blank.

It's hard for me—even today—to acknowledge that compared to my mother, my father was the healthy one.

Chapter 7

Reality Check

JUNIOR HIGH

As I compiled my notes and records in preparation for writing this book, I wondered why I had kept certain mementos and discarded others. I had saved two faded pages of wide-ruled, lined paper on which fifty-three junior-high kids had signed a petition. Addressed to my mother in my handwriting, it reads: "It is very important that you reconsider and let Julie go to Disneyland on April 18th under Mrs. Johnson's* strict supervision! It is a fundamental step in making her a well-rounded person and in increasing her knowledge. Thank you for your understanding and co-operation!"

I cherished it because it was proof of *a time when I won.* Although my mother had said I could not go on the group trip, she changed her mind after receiving the petition. Maybe other mothers talked with her? Maybe she didn't want it known that she was the only parent who had refused to allow her child to participate?

We lived on a Marine Corps base in southern California. These somewhat normal years were sandwiched between the childhood sexual abuse and the upcoming pressures for achievement and popularity in high school. We junior high kids did bowling, swimming, golfing, basketball, horseback riding and sleepovers and went to a lot of movies. All the activities were inexpensive and

---

*   Real person; fictionalized name

I was allowed to participate. Most of my memories from seventh through ninth grades are of fun times with friends—"Cyndi," "Jolee," "Suzanne" and "Karen."

School was always a safe haven. I did school well. I recall one special teacher from those years—Mr. Probe—who was smart and kind and thought that I was, too. I had him for math for at least two years in row. It became my favorite subject.

After ninth grade, my father retired from the military and we moved back to mother's hometown of Eugene, Oregon. My father got a job, mother bought a house and I went to school and tried to make them proud of me.

THE NO-KNOCK RULE

Mother no longer touched me in sexual ways—not unless you count that she would sometimes still kiss me on the mouth. I hated that. Throughout my high school years, her behaviors were more subtle and covert:

1) She continued to intentionally expose herself to me by calling me into her bathroom when she was bathing or on the toilet. She would beseech me, "Come here, honey—come tell me all about your day while I'm in the tub."

I would try to put her off. "I'm busy now," I'd call back, or I'd say, "Let me know when you're out and we can visit then, Mother." Sometimes that worked; most of the time it didn't.

When forced to be in the bathroom with her, I would try to divert my eyes from her naked body. That would anger her. "You can look at me, Missy. There's nothing to be ashamed of between mother and daughter. I have a beautiful body."

She would not stay under water in the tub. She made sure to arch herself up out of the water to wash her "privates" with a wash-cloth while I was in the bathroom. I would look away and try to keep talking so she wouldn't notice my inattention. It was hell.

Sometimes she would call for me when she had to use the toilet. When I got to her bedroom, she would enter their adjoining bath-room and insist that I sit and talk with her while she was having a bowel movement. "I'm going to be here awhile so let's chat," she'd say. Oh, wonderful, I thought.

2) Worse, however, was her pre-occupation with menstruation cycles—hers *and* mine. She insisted on knowing dates and details of my periods; she freely shared information about her periods with me. She even went so far as to show me her soiled sanitary pads and to want to see mine—"to see if you're doing OK…just to be sure you're fine." In total disgust, I silently obeyed.

With both horror and relief I've read about other mothers' identical behaviors in Rosencrans' book (1997). While I was heartbroken that anyone else had to experience what I had, it was also validating to know that I wasn't the only one. Watching their daughters or forcing their daughters to watch them during bathing, toileting, dressing and undressing seem to be common behavior patterns of mother-daughter incest.

3) I had no privacy. No locks on my doors. Mother would enter my room or bathroom whenever she desired. If I were getting dressed or undressed, she would plop down on my bed and start talking, all the while staring at my body. She wanted to know my weight; she wanted to know my bra size. She needed to see me naked or semi-naked.

I was so naïve; our mother-daughter relationship was my only frame of reference.

She had established these norms of physical and psychological intimacy during my early childhood; it had been like this with her forever. Now that I was older and it felt so humiliating and wrong, I didn't know what else to do. My protests were in vain.

"You're my daughter, honey," she would say. "There's nothing we two can't share. That's just how it is."

There were trade-offs. If I wanted any freedom—to use the telephone, to go on a date, to attend a school dance, to spend the night with a girlfriend—I knew I had to please her. She never came out and said, "Let me watch you undress and you can go to the movies." It wasn't that blatant, of course. But if she did not like my "attitude" that week, she would suspend my privileges.

She judged my attitude based on my grades in school, how well I did my chores (dishes, ironing, etc.), my compliance with her daily requests for gossip about other kids at school *and* how well I handled her requests for private "mother-daughter time." Particular weight was given to the last item.

Bottom line: I was afraid of her. I tried to do whatever she requested to keep her happy. Years later, I asked myself what exactly had I feared at that time? What did I think she would do if I displeased her? Slap me? Sure—but she did that occasionally anyway. Restrict me? I was used to that. Hurt me? Kill me? I did not consciously believe that. Yet, I always had an inner sense not to cross this woman.

4) She had strange conversations with me about sex. Sometimes she would confide in me, sharing intimate details about her physical relationship (or the lack thereof) with my father. This always made me extremely uncomfortable.

Sometimes she made it sound as if having sex was a horrific experience to be avoided at all costs. She talked about men contemptuously because "they really like sex." "Maybe you'll get lucky like I did and get one who doesn't care so much about it," she once disclosed.

HIGH SCHOOL DAZE

I did not realize how restricted my high school years were until I visited with former classmates decades later at our high school reunions. I never went to any of the teenage "hang-outs" (except for a popular pizza parlor with girlfriends), never went to even one boy-girl party at someone's home and I usually had to be home shortly after every football game. I immersed myself in activities that kept me busy after school—the debate team, the newspaper staff, drama club (working behind the scenes). If it served to postpone my going home, I volunteered for it.

I had two best girlfriends who remain cherished, lifelong friends to this day. Even though I didn't tell them much about my mother at the time (nobody talked about sexual abuse back then), the hours I was allowed to spend with them were life saving.

I do remember sometimes going to the "Stomp"—teen dances the city sponsored on Saturday nights—with girlfriends and I *was* allowed to go on some dates. Mother tried to research each boy first. She was more concerned with the boy's looks, popularity and the family social standing than what kind of person he might be. Still, I did go out with several nice, fun and interesting guys. Little did I know at the time that she was keeping that list of my boyfriends' names (with special symbols indicating only God knows what), just as she had kept the chart of her own suitors years before.

Puzzlingly, I remember little of my high school years. A former classmate approached my husband and me at our most recent reunion in 2005 and jokingly asked why I would never go out with him in high school. He said he called and called and I always turned him down. I was dumbfounded.

I remembered him clearly and how I *had* liked him—he was outgoing and cute and seemed very nice—yet I don't remember ever taking a single phone call from him. Did my mother intercept his phone calls, pretending that she was me? (I know that sounds crazy but, for her, not impossible.) Did he call but I declined because I assumed it was a joke—because he was such a handsome, popular guy? Did I say "no" to spare him from having to meet my parents? *How could I have just forgotten?*

Mother tried repeatedly to fix me up with the sons of some of her old high school and college friends. We would visit their families in other Oregon towns or she would invite them to our home. Those who had money and connections and were bound for Ivy League schools were deemed worthy of her daughter's virtue, literally. While I was not supposed to even kiss boys from my school, she made it clear that there were no such rules when it came to snaring one of these fine "catches." Alas, the boys were fun and respectful; we were just friends. Mother was disappointed in me.

Mother taught me her very special wardrobe secrets when I was in high school. She had two clothing rules:

1) Never wear purple; only whores wear purple. (I didn't know whether or not lavender counted but I never purchased clothing in either color until I was in my thirties.)

2) Rotate your wardrobe! She kept precise records of when she wore which outfits to church, what she wore to bridge club and what she wore to other club meetings so that she could rotate her clothing. Then people would not remember her being in a particular outfit. The goal was for people to think she had more clothes than she did.

Mother insisted that I keep a list of which outfits I wore to school each day. I, too, was to rotate through my list in precise order. By wearing outfits as far apart as possible, it would appear that I, too, had more clothes. So, I'd wake up Monday morning and feel like wearing my favorite green printed dress, which was clean, ironed and hanging in my closet. Couldn't do it! I'd already worn it last Thursday. I would have to wait until the following week so that the other girls would not have seen it for a while.

I used to wonder if other mothers were like her. I would watch other teenage girls with their moms in restaurants or shopping together in department stores and try to determine how genuine their smiles were. Were others really enjoying being together or was it forced? My mother acted friendly in public. I wondered if everyone was just acting and things changed once these other women arrived back home, too.

I was a junior in high school when President Kennedy was assassinated in the Fall of 1963. I clearly remember when the announcement came over our school's public address system. When I got home, we watched the news but we did not talk. My father told me to quit crying because there was nothing I could do about it. No discussion.

The Civil Rights Act was passed in June 1964. That same month, Michael Schwerner, James Chaney and Andy Goodman, three civil rights activists helping with voter registration in Mississippi, were beaten, shot and killed by the Ku Klux Klan. I learned about their murders on the evening news, but no discussion was allowed.

My father said, "We're not going to talk about it. Those damn nigger-lover, civil rights workers should have been home minding their own business. It's their own fault they got killed."

During the Spring of my senior year, March 7th, 1965 the Southern Christian Leadership Conference attempted to march from Selma to Montgomery, Alabama. The evening news showed the marchers being attacked and beaten. The United States also sent combat troops to Vietnam and began the bombings in 1965.

These important, significant world-changing events were taking place during my high school years. At school, we discussed them. At lunch with friends, we discussed them. At home, at our dinner table and in our living room, we pretended that nothing was happening. "Don't worry your little head about any of this stuff," my father said, dismissing both my questions and my moral outrage. Mother described the setting of her latest bridge match and gossiped endlessly about those in attendance and those not. When it became too surreal, I'd find myself checking out.

I cannot remember a time when I ever "fit in" with my own family. (Although now I realize that not fitting in wasn't such a bad thing.) I cannot remember a time when I didn't feel "different" from all the other girls at school. I didn't know why I was different but I knew it was *not* a good thing.

DIVINE INTERVENTION

Thank God I was accepted at an out-of-town college! My two choices were to live at home and attend the University of Oregon or go away to the smaller, private, more expensive (to my mother this meant "prestigious") church-affiliated Willamette University in Salem, Oregon. It was less than an hour's drive away but it was *away*.

I almost flunked out first semester. Freshman usually enrolled in biology; I had decided to take geology instead, even though I didn't have the recommended pre-requisite math background. It was a disastrous decision earning me four semester hours of "F." I didn't do well in my other classes either—my illustrious college career began with a 1.56 grade point average. My only distinction this first semester was qualifying for "academic probation." But by the following summer, I was off probation and holding my own.

Despite my poor grades, I learned a lot that year. I learned that my home life was strange and stifling when compared to the other girls' families. The other girls' letters from their moms read nothing like mine—theirs were uplifting and supportive. As I gradually began to discover how different my parents were, I chastised myself for not realizing it sooner. I was dismayed at my own naïveté. I became depressed, which led me to ditch classes, go for long walks alone, binge on junk food, and stay up late reading *and* writing dark poetry.

But I also took two sophomore-level philosophy and ethics courses as a freshman and then two junior-level "History of Philosophy" classes during my sophomore year. The "B's" and "C's" I earned in those classes meant more to me than "A's" in any other. I was encouraged to think and to reason—two activities that had been discouraged in my parents' home.

The lessons I learned the two years I spent at that university would sustain and empower me throughout my life:

1) *I was not garbage.* I met some kind-hearted, fun, bright students and teachers who seemed to like me, whether I was failing classes or earning a few A's and B's. Who was I to question their judgment?

2) *I could learn and achieve.* I wasn't stupid or hopeless. My grades improved dramatically when I took appropriate courses, learned how to study and attended class.

3) *I did not have to join a sorority to have a happy life.* Mother had been wrong about that, too.

4) *Staying as far away as possible from my toxic family was a healthy thing.*

Something extraordinary happened at the end of my freshman year. The campus pastor-religion professor recommended me for a camp-counselor job with the Methodist church, summer-youth program. It turned out to be one of the most affirming experiences of my life and the forerunner to a counseling career.

At first I was apprehensive that I would need to memorize the books of the Bible or know all about bugs and leaves. Instead, it was a new type of experiential Christian camp featuring "sensitivity group" activities that focused on communication skills and personal growth. Mostly we talked with and listened to kids. We worked with elementary school kids one week and junior high the next; we rotated between a mountain site and a coastal location. We talked about a compassionate God who wanted them to become their best selves and to be kind and caring to others.

The camp director and his wife offered me my first glimpse of how emotionally healthy adults could interact in the world. They were calm and loving, non-judgmental and fun—so patient with the children. They took me under their wings, too. At the summer's end, they drove me home. Although I had tried to describe my parents for them, nothing could have prepared them for the actual meeting. I still have a letter that they wrote me in January of 1968. I was to treasure their validation for all time:

"...I understand fully your feelings about your home situation—the difference between you and your parents was painful for me to witness even for the brief moments we were there. Our hearts really went out for you... ."

Following two years at Willamette, in 1967 I transferred to the University of Oregon. The reasons were largely financial. I'd grown weary of mother's letters complaining of all their monetary sacrifices for me. Because the public university would cost considerably less, my parents gave in and let me live in a dormitory on campus.

But during that summer of '67, I had little choice but to spend ten weeks living at home. I enrolled in summer classes at the university and I rode my bike to school every day. I tried to just stay on campus as much as possible. In August I moved into a coed dormitory. I would never again live in my parents' house nor be totally under their control.

MARRIAGE, MOTHERHOOD AND THE MIDWEST

During my junior year, I saw as little as possible of my parents. I enjoyed my classes as an English major, life in the dorm, a part-time job on campus and a serious relationship with the man I would soon marry. He was a teaching assistant and doctoral candidate in economics and the antithesis of my father—intelligent, non-militaristic, non-racist, non-judgmental, thoughtful, with a wry wit. It was a terrific year of challenging coursework, late-night discussions, graduate-student parties and falling in love.

When he took me out of state to meet his parents, I was pleased, both that they were so kind-hearted and that he actually wanted them to meet *me*. I hoped somehow that they would never have to meet my mother and father.

In August 1968 we learned that I was pregnant; he proposed on the way home from the doctor's office.

We told my parents. My father called me a whore. They refused to attend our little chapel wedding, even after I telephoned them the night before and begged them to please come. I was sentenced to a lifetime of shame and guilt. My crimes? Having sex before marriage, getting pregnant which would let everyone know that I'd had sex and spoiling mother's plans for me to marry into a family of wealth, status and power. By wedding a common, struggling grad student, I had ruined *her* one remaining chance for improving her social standing in the community. *That* was unforgivable.

Conversely, upon hearing our news, my future husband's parents immediately gave us their blessing. His mom even asked about my health. They sent us money for our wedding present. We bought some inexpensive redwood "patio furniture" for our little living room and moved into student housing over Labor Day weekend. I quit my job and loaded up on credits so I could graduate the following Spring, just before the baby was due. We were in shock, overwhelmed, but happy.

Mother feigned support for me in public, even to the point of attending a baby shower hosted by one of her friends. Privately, she remained hateful. She telephoned in December, when I was five months along, to say that there was still a chance that I could lose my baby. "Your auntie in San Francisco miscarried at five months, you know, so you could too," she said, *hopefully.* "Then people would never even have to know you'd been pregnant." She meant her friends—like her bridge buddies who might gossip about us the same way that she consistently scandalized them. I wept.

In March 1969 I received my B.A. degree in English from the University of Oregon. My mother talked me out of going through the ceremonies. After all, everyone would *know* I was pregnant. (At nine months, I think so.) She thought it would be too embarrassing. (For whom, I wondered?)

Two weeks later, our beautiful, healthy son was born. In August we moved over a thousand miles away for my husband's first university teaching job and to begin a new life in the Midwest. I would take adult driver-education classes and pass my driver's license exam the next year.

I admit that I did not view blizzards as blessings at the time. But we would spend fourteen years on the prairie, and my children and I would remain safely distanced from my mother. Well, for the most part.

COUNSELING 101

I called the Mental Health Center the day after Christmas, 1973. I was crashing. I don't remember the exact cause of my "holiday blues" but the focus was always my parents. It may have been long-held sorrow over my childhood Christmases or it could have been something more current.

Sometimes my parents didn't like my gifts and would make a point of sending them back to me. One year I bought my mother a big, overstuffed corduroy-covered molded pillow so she could sit up and read in bed. She had said she liked to do that. She let me know that she thought it was "ugly" and "an awkward shape," and she shipped it back to me.

My father forever critiqued my gift-wrapping and shipping skills. Nothing I sent them ever got lost or trashed in the mail but he worried excessively about the possibility. "Use more strapping tape, Missy," he would say. "Didn't you learn anything from watching me?" To this day, my children gently tease me about my obsessive taping. It is still frightening to me whenever I knowingly break one of my father's rules.

The psychiatrist I met with was an interesting fellow. He barely looked at me during our hour together. He seemed more focused on prolific note taking. He interrupted me with quick-fired questions, "So, what do you call your mother-in-law?" (No, I don't think *she* is my mother.)

He asked about my childhood. "I really don't remember too much before the age of nine," I said. I intentionally downplayed my parents' bizarre behaviors. It felt disloyal and frightening to discuss them at all. I minimized any maltreatment, but he was skilled and able to fill in some of the blanks.

I met with him only that one time. He gave me sound advice, some of which I even acted upon. He said something to the effect that my parents were unhealthy and that I should formally separate from them forever. Of course I did not do that but just hearing his perception of them was powerful for me.

He also said that I needed to find something for *me*—he suggested going back to school or getting a job or pursuing a hobby. I was twenty-six and a full-time mom with a four-year-old son and a one-year-old daughter. I told him that I couldn't possibly do that until my youngest child was in school—maybe in five years. He said, "You don't have to wait that long." He was right, but it took me awhile to believe him.

Fall semester, 1974 I enrolled in a graduate course entitled, "Fundamentals of Counseling." The subject was intriguing and the class was offered on evenings when my husband could tend our children alone. Walking into the first class session, apprehensive and insecure, little did I know I had just found my calling.

Busy with my children and some volunteer tutoring, I did not return to graduate school until spring, 1976. For the following two years I took classes (mostly evenings) and completed twenty-hours-per-week counseling internships while simultaneously parenting, teaching Sunday school, serving on the PTA board and co-leading our son's Cub Scout troop. My husband was supportive in word and deed; my weekends were often spent in the library or using the typewriter in his campus office. I received my Master's in Counseling and Guidance in May 1978, graduating with a 3.9 grade point average. *This time* I went through the ceremonies with my children and husband cheering from the stands.

In August, I started a part-time counseling job; I left that position during the 1980-81 school year to complete the requirements for my state school counseling credential. From August 1981 through May 2004, I was privileged to work with middle school and high school students as their school counselor. I tried to provide them the same healthy support that several adults had given to me and to instill in them the belief that they were worthy of happiness and success. Some days I even believed that *I* was.

THE LIST

Whenever I counseled kids from severely troubled families, I often asked them if they were keeping a list. Their responses were sometimes skeptical at first, "What list?" they'd ask, defiantly. "How did you know?" they might question, in disbelief. I was referring to "the list of the things I will do differently if I have kids some day." I gently told them, "I know because when I was a kid, I always had my list going in my head, too. And you know what? I've been able to stick to it. If I could do it, you can, too."

If they were aware enough to construct a list, there was hope. They were stepping back—separating from their parents, looking at the behaviors—and taking a stand. Near the top of every single kid's list, and of my own, was some statement about not calling kids names or swearing at them or putting kids down.

At first, I worried because I had no healthy parenting model to replicate. I soon discovered that I had an excellent model—a model of what *not* to do. Based on my "list," I tried to recall or envision what my parents would have done in different situations, and then I'd do the most opposite thing I could imagine. For example, as a child, I would have been lectured and whacked for not drinking all my milk. With my own kids, it was never an issue. I might give them only half as much milk the next time and explain that they could always ask for more. No big deal.

Some days I was not a very mature parent. I lost patience and yelled when my kids were just being kids. I was ignorant about how to handle ordinary sibling conflicts so I relied heavily on my husband's perspective from his more normal childhood experiences. I knew not to beat them or call them hurtful names, but I was often at a loss of what to do instead. So, we laughed a lot. Their dad was a wonderful father—loving and patient—with them. They were terrific kids who grew into healthy, well-adjusted, productive adults.

When my kids were young, I confess that sometimes I had bizarre thoughts of things I could do to them. I recall thinking how I could confuse them if I taught them the wrong colors—for example, that black was orange and red was really blue. Then they'd be ridiculed at school. I felt the enormous power that parents have over their children.

Occasionally I had sexual fantasies about my own children. This is painful for me to acknowledge even now. I was horrified. I chastised myself for having such disgusting thoughts. "Where could those thoughts be coming from?" I would ask myself. I had no desire to act upon the ideas but the shame and guilt I felt for even imagining sexual acts with children overwhelmed me. I told no one. I assumed the images somehow stemmed from my own inherent badness. After all, my father had always told me that I was crazy.

NOT WITH MY CHILD, YOU DON'T!

My parents came to visit us in December 1977 for a Midwestern "White Christmas." I don't remember much of what we did— whether we went to church or out to eat or shopping. However, what did happen that visit so shocked me that it eclipsed anything else of their stay.

My kids were young. My son—eight years old, third grade,

busy with ice hockey and Cub Scouts and building snow forts with his friends—a gentle soul. His sister—five, a kindergartener, trying her best to keep up with him and his buddies—a "tough little cookie."

One morning I was making breakfast for everyone. I could hear my daughter, my husband and my father interacting in the living room. I wondered where my son was. He was usually the first one in the kitchen, eager to help me.

I called his name and heard a faint, distant reply. "I'm in here, Mommy." I bolted down the hallway to our bedroom, the room that my parents were using during their visit. I flung open the door. My fifty-eight-year-old mother was in her underwear. My son stood there wide-eyed, frozen with fear.

He ran to me. I hugged him and mumbled something like, "Let's go fix breakfast," and scooted him out of the room. My blood boiled. I looked back at her in disbelief and disgust. "I was just getting *dressed*," she said, with feigned innocence. "There's nothing to be ashamed of between grandparents and grandchildren." Now, a chill ran down my spine. Echoes of the past. I thought, *"Not with my child you don't."* I hurried out to be with my son.

After that, I consciously kept my son and daughter safely distanced from my mother. As a mother grizzly bear might protect her cubs, I was watchful of her every interaction with them.

That Christmas memory lingered long and deep in my psyche. After my mother's death in 1983, when the recollections of *my* early sexual abuse came back, I vividly remembered the episode with my son. Yet I had never brought it up. I told myself, he probably doesn't even remember it. I hoped I'd imagined it. Or maybe I'd exaggerated it? How could I know for sure?

Visiting my son and his wife in 2004, I shared my plans to write this book. After twenty-seven years of silence, I took a deep breath and finally asked him, "Do you remember anything that happened with your grandmother when you were a little boy?"

"Yeah," he said, immediately recalling what I was referring to. "The time grandma called me into her room and she didn't have her clothes on. Oh yes, I remember."

Chapter 8

From Victim to Survivor

DISENGAGEMENT

When parents are evil—when they abuse their child sexually and emotionally—at some point the child must consciously reject the perpetrators. I believe that in order to survive psychologically, a victim must come to the conclusion that "I am OK but the adults I live with (lived with) are sick."

It can take years, or decades, or a lifetime for victims to accomplish this *fundamental psychological separation from their abusers*. But until this separation occurs, victims will remain stuck—conflicted about love and sex and family and power—struggling with issues of self-worth and self-respect. Victims who remain emotionally crippled are at risk for depression, self-injury, suicide, chemical dependency, academic and employment failure, repeated sexual victimization, early parenthood *and* for either abusing their own children themselves or for not protecting them from harm by others.

As long as victims still identify with their perpetrators, minimize the abuse, make excuses for their parents and deny the degree of harm inflicted, *they* will not be emotionally healthy or safe with children. There has to be a conscious separation—a declaration to the Universe, if you will—that says, "I am not like them and I will not be!"

Yet, a common response to mother-child incest that is particularly problematic for separation and healing is repression. How can victims confront experiences that they don't fully remember or report abusive behavior that they had long presumed to be normal?

Mental health professionals—from school counselors and social workers to psychiatrists—must become aware of the family dynamics that enable mother-child molestation to occur. Young boys and girls must be encouraged to describe their home life experiences, even if they aren't presenting themselves as victims or reporting sexual abuse at the time. We can help them to see themselves as separate human beings who can become healthy, caring adults, regardless of their family situations.

Counselors readily support kids in differentiating themselves from their drug-dealing older siblings or their fathers incarcerated for spousal abuse. We praise kids for making different, more constructive choices for themselves. We need also to affirm students struggling to make philosophical breaks from their troubled families, even when the parents may "look good" on the surface.

If we allow students to create that "list of the things I will do differently if I have kids some day," we not only affirm their individuality but also learn more about their private worlds. Students typically write such things as, "I won't make my kids do their homework when there's a game on TV." More revealing, however, is the girl who declares, "I won't walk in on my daughter when she's taking a bath" or the boy who writes, "I won't make my son sleep with his mom when I'm out of town."

Kids can't and don't easily disclose mother-child incest. It is hard for them to tell about any type of abuse, let alone something sexual with their *mother*. But "the list" is a starting place to talk about behaviors in their homes that make them uncomfortable or ashamed or embarrassed. The list is a non-threatening way to increase their self-awareness and healthy individuality. It also gives the counselor a new understanding of the family dynamics and may offer warning signs of maternal sexual abuse.

We must not exclude females as potential perpetrators in our educational and prevention programs; kids need to know that some adolescent girls and some women *do* molest children. Youngsters need to hear about covert sexually abusive behaviors. If nobody ever tells them it's wrong, how can they get the behavior stopped? How can victims of mother-child incest ask for help if nobody acknowledges that sexually abusive females even exist?

Blue Sky Bridge, a Child and Family Advocacy Program in Boulder, Colorado offers educational programs as well as direct services for child sexual-assault victims and their non-offending family members. Posted on their website is an excellent article entitled, "What to Watch for When Adults Play with Children." It is no accident that both male and female pronouns are used throughout its listing of warning signs. This change from the single-sex language that usually implies that all perpetrators are male is significant. Example: "Spends most of his or her spare time with children and has little interest in spending time with someone his or her own age?"

Two more of the warning signs highlight covert behaviors often present in mother-child incest: "Frequently walks in on children or teens in the bathroom?" and "Is overly interested in the sexuality of a particular child or teen (e.g. talks repeatedly about the child's developing body or interferes with normal teen dating)?" (Appendix D.) (Note: information in the Blue Sky Bridge article "comes from the *National Child Advocate*, Vol. 5, No .2.")

Society tends to excuse the behavior and minimize its impact whenever the perpetrator is female. The media nearly always portray a gentler, kinder molester when the rapist is a woman. Recently, however, there have been notable exceptions.

In November 2005, Margaret De Barraicua, a thirty-year-old teacher intern in Sacramento, California was found guilty of the statutory rape of her male sixteen-year-old special education student. "De Barraicua was originally charged with four felony counts of statutory rape. In an earlier court appearance her attorney, Phil Cozens, said his client was remorseful and proposed reducing the charges to misdemeanors. Prosecutors rejected that proposal." She was sentenced to a year in jail and five years probation. (Bishop. November 18, 2005. *Sacramento News 10*.)

Numerous friends and relatives had addressed the court on De Barraicua's behalf. They described her as a community volunteer, a philanthropist, a devout Catholic and a loving mother. A local pastor and family friend defended her and believed the teenager should share some responsibility. "His consensual decision to participate in this encounter should be accountable," the minister said. Police had caught her having sex with her special-needs student in the front seat of her car. Her two-year-old son was strapped into his safety seat in the rear of the car at the time. (Coronado. July 7, 2005. *Sacramento Bee.*)

Also in November 2005, Silvia Johnson, forty-one, pleaded guilty to two misdemeanor sex-assault counts and nine felony counts of contributing to the delinquency of a minor for providing teenage boys with alcohol and other drugs and having sex with them. She wanted to be a "cool mom." A Colorado judge sentenced her to thirty years in prison. (Nicholson. November 15, 2005. *Denver Post.*)

Although the media is reporting more incidents of women sexually assaulting children, most of these cases have involved females in their twenties or thirties having sex with adolescent boys—illegal and wrong—but still fodder for late-night television monologues. For most people to believe that mothers molest their own young (and sometimes not so young) children requires a huge leap of thought. With some distorted sense of logic they may regard mother-son and mother-daughter incest as somehow more tender and therefore less harmful. They could not be more wrong! While mothers' incestuous behaviors are often more covert, the emotional and psychological damage is just as severe as in father-daughter sexual abuse.

THE FLOODGATES OPEN

We had moved from the Midwest to Colorado in July of 1983—just prior to my mother's death that August. Autumn found us adjusting to new jobs, new schools, a new house and a milder climate. I was busy taking care of my children and husband and learning

137

procedures and responsibilities in a new high school work setting; I did not want to spend time or energy dealing with memories of my childhood abuse.

But the flashbacks to my childhood experiences grew in frequency and intensity over the next five years. After the excruciatingly vivid recollection of forced enemas surfaced during my summer 1987 hysterectomy hospitalization, the memory floodgates seemed to stay open. Sometimes I tried to stop the flow of intrusive thoughts and images by concentrating extra hard on work and distracting myself with new projects and programs at school. Occasionally that strategy worked.

The 1987-88 school year proved to be a time of overwhelming professional and personal challenge. I switched counseling jobs. The middle-school counselor whom I replaced was a beloved long-term member of the faculty and well known in the community. His retirement was highly publicized in the local newspaper. A few months later, his arrest, release and suicide would also make the front page.

This man had sexually abused at least one boy, outside of the school setting. Parents trusted him and appreciated his interest in their sons; group sleepovers, camping trips and social events at his home were common. He had been "grooming" boys for sexual activity through inappropriate touch and game activities in what was now *my* counseling office at school. Kids told me all about it.

A painful, chaotic whirlwind engulfed the school. I was the new, unknown counselor who had reported the crimes committed by a cherished member of "the school family." Even though the police had documentation—a confessional letter he had written to a victim—many of his former colleagues were too overwhelmed to accept the truth of what this man had done. Understandably, some seemed to blame me for their pain. Guilt devastated other staff members who blamed themselves for not seeing what had been happening—and not even knowing what to have looked for. It was the worst of times.

Certain elements of his abuse—deception, betrayal and secrecy—bombarded me emotionally unlike any other case in my counseling career. In previous years I had filed sexual abuse reports with Social Services, including incest, but I was always able to somehow insulate myself from any intense personal reactions. Not this time. Nightmares and flashbacks relentlessly interfered as I tried to function and just get through each day. A full night's sleep eluded me. Sometimes I could not stand to be touched. The school community was gradually healing but I wasn't. In April of 1988, after six months of flashbacks and confusion, I finally acknowledged that I needed help and I sought therapy.

"WALKING WOUNDED"

Perhaps no greater betrayal exists than that of mother-daughter or mother-son incest. Although victims have the devastating experience of maternal betrayal in common, their understanding of the abuse and their individual responses to it can vary greatly. Each person has a unique history that leads her or him into therapy.

A man whose mother molested him may struggle with puzzling, lifelong depression and an endless string of broken relationships. Another may excel in the business world by day but turn to alcohol at night to numb his "crazy feelings." Victims of mother-daughter incest could be found prostituting themselves on a street corner in Las Vegas or performing on stage with The New York City Ballet. Some adult incest victims will have careers in law enforcement; others may be the career criminals.

If they seek counseling help, their initial reason for seeing a therapist is often depression or sleep disturbances or relationship problems, not necessarily their memories of maternal abuse. While they may wear their hearts on their sleeves, the cause of their angst is often deeply hidden.

Years ago, I heard the term, "walking wounded." It resonated with me. I recently looked it up online:

1. casualties who can walk: casualties of war, terrorism, or disaster who are able to walk despite their injuries and

2. people who have been hurt: people who continue to be affected by great emotional pain experienced during their

lives (MSN Encarta online dictionary)

The term well describes all adults who were sexually abused by their mothers. Until we receive help, we each remain crippled to some degree, in one way or another.

SIX CRITICAL ISSUES FOR THERAPY

Victims develop a variety of strategies for coping with the incest and its impact on their lives. What individual clients need from therapy varies greatly, as will their therapists' expertise in the area of mother-child sexual abuse. From my experience, most of these issues need to be addressed with both male and female victims of maternal abuse.

1) *Belief.* Victims don't usually seek therapy for maternal incest until adulthood, after they have left home and the sexual abuse has stopped. Even if they have clear, concrete memories, they are understandably convinced that nobody would believe them. If they attempted to tell a friend or relative, in all likelihood they were met with skepticism or revulsion. Such victims enter therapy with *two fears: (1) that the counselor will not believe them and (2) that the counselor will believe them. What then?*

Society has made great strides in acknowledging that incest does occur and more frequently than we like to think—but with male perpetrators. The 1984 groundbreaking prime-time movie, "Something About Amelia," was the first film to show a nice, all-American family that included an incestuous father. Ted Danson earned a Golden Globe award for his portrayal of the handsome, clean cut, intelligent perpetrator-dad, and Glenn Close was his unsuspecting wife. At fourteen, Roxana Zal earned an Emmy Award for her portrayal of the daughter who was victimized. (Internet Movie Database)

We watched it as a family. I revealed nothing. I recall the discussions in the high-school teachers' lounge the next day. "Do you think that really happens?" they'd ask me, since I was a counselor. "But surely not in nice families like that?"

Disbelief about female perpetrators, specifically mothers, is even more common. Among personal acquaintances and even mental-health professionals, I sometimes receive responses of skepticism or shock when I begin to tell my story. When they react by breaking eye contact or with vile expressions and involuntary shuddering, our dialogue ends. If a therapist's demeanor conveys disgust or incredulity at the first hint of mother-daughter sexual activity, the client may cease all genuine disclosure.

Mother-daughter incest is the most rarely reported form of sexual abuse. This may be in part due to mental-health-professionals' lack of knowledge about maternal sexual abuse and their lack of experience in supporting clients to self-disclose. It is extremely difficult for victims to disclose mother-child sexual abuse, given the horrific stigma that accompanies maternal incest. I once spoke with a fellow conference attendee—a psychologist who had been in private practice for over a decade—who said he had never worked with an incest survivor, period. When he said his clientele was mostly females, ages thirty to fifty, I replied, "Oh yes, you have." "Well, they never divulged it to me," he said, seeming somewhat puzzled.

Victims of maternal incest may not want to admit that they *were* sexually abused. Covert sexual behaviors must be identified and labeled as sexually abusive acts willfully perpetrated by their mothers. This process is both excruciating and cathartic. Although it hurt to finally acknowledge that my own mother had sexually abused me for years, it was sanity saving for me to *know* once and for all that I was not crazy. The things she did to me were morally wrong; my reactions and responses were normal and sane. Victims must come to believe that they had no choice. They were forced to comply and none of the abuse was their fault. The guilt can be overpowering. I felt guilty for:

- letting it happen, not getting away; not physically fighting my mother
- being stupid and not even knowing it was wrong
- not telling anyone at the time

- not fully remembering for years
- not talking about it with my own kids (even if I had not known what "it" was)
- staying in the home and not running away at sixteen or seventeen
- not confronting her
- being compliant
- trusting her
- thinking evil, vengeful thoughts
- not totally severing the relationship
- telling our secrets even now
- ultimately, being born.

Cognitive therapy helped me (1) to understand why incest victims often don't tell, (2) to recognize and to accept the helpless child I had been and (3) to celebrate the coping strategies I had used to survive. I was in weekly therapy for six months.

Learning that the coping mechanisms I had used were fairly typical of incest victims helped me to normalize my reactions. I was not crazy—I had done what I needed to do to survive psychologically. It was time to re-frame: the dissociation and repression were not pathological responses but were normal, rational reactions to overwhelming trauma. Sometimes remembering is overrated. I would come to say, "I am thankful that I checked out. Thank God I stuffed a lot of this for all those years."

2) *Betrayal and loss.* Realizing that my perpetrator was my mother was more devastating to me than remembering any specific acts of abuse. The *who* was more problematic to accept than the *what;* the *why* was more mystifying than the *how.*

Why would my own mother molest me? As I recalled incident after incident of inappropriate words and deeds, her face and voice stayed in my mind. Her sloppy, red mouth came at me again as I struggled to sidestep each embrace. "Mommy just loves you so much," she murmured as she reached for me across the bed. What I found unpardonable was the lifelong deception—her intentional misrepresentation of our mother-daughter relationship as normal and healthy and loving. That violated the most sacred of trusts.

When I read a review of Jennifer J. Freyd's book, *Betrayal Trauma: The Logic of Forgetting Childhood Abuse,* in a 1997 University of Oregon publication, I hurried out to purchase a copy. I knew that I had repressed many childhood experiences. Some of my memories had spontaneously returned just after my mother's death. Other recollections surfaced shortly before and during the time I was in therapy. Even in the 1990's, occasionally a new scene from my childhood would appear, momentarily overpowering me with the images, the sounds and those feelings from my past.

I struggled to comprehend how and why I could have bottled up such dreadful experiences for so many years. Logic dictated—or so I had thought—that people would forever and clearly remember bizarre, horrific incidents of child abuse. I mistakenly likened the trauma of child sexual abuse to that of experiencing a natural disaster or the death of the beloved family pet. My own children could vividly recall the Midwest tornado sightings of their youth, so why couldn't I remember my mother's touch?

Freyd stated:

> Betrayal trauma theory proposes that the traumas that are most likely to be forgotten are not necessarily the most painful, terrifying, or overwhelming ones (although they may have those qualities), but the traumas in which betrayal is a fundamental component. This proposition points to the central role of social relationships in traumas that are forgotten.

> Interpersonal traumas, such as domestic abuse and child abuse, are clearly examples of social traumas that possess components of betrayal, especially in cases where the perpetrator is a trusted and intimate person in the life of the victim. The more the victim is dependent on the perpetra-

tor—the more power the perpetrator has over the victim in a trusted and intimate relationship—the more the crime is one of betrayal. This betrayal by a trusted caregiver is the core factor in determining amnesia for a trauma. (1996, pp. 62-63)

Freyd maintains that children who are dependent on their parents (or other caregivers) for food, shelter and basic needs must block out their awareness of being betrayed to continue to get along with those caregivers. The consequences of challenging their caregiver-perpetrator could be life threatening. "In other words, in order to survive in cases of core betrayals (abuse by a trusted caregiver on a dependent victim) some amount of information blockage is likely to be required." (1996, p. 75)

My mother made it clear that she was in control. If pet turtles and a baby chicken could die, I reasoned, so, too, could a little girl or, at best, get her tongue cut out for telling. It now makes perfect sense that I would "forget" most of the abuse until after she was dead. I would be compliant, well behaved, quiet and obedient and, if anyone asked, would deny that there were any problems at home. But back then, nobody ever asked.

So frightening is the betrayal of maternal abuse that the victim often represses much of the incestuous behavior until after the perpetrator has died. Bobbie Rosencrans, wrote, "My clinical experience indicates that some daughters enter psychotherapy around the time their mothers die. Many of the daughters in this study commented on issues surrounding their feelings regarding the deaths of their abusive mothers." (1997, p. 233)

"It was the biggest relief of my life," wrote one adult victim cited in Rosencrans' book. "I realized it almost immediately and expected some guilt to hit me for feeling that way but it's been almost ten years now and that's all it ever was. Just a big relief. I've slept better since then." (1997, p. 233)

Another survivor of maternal incest wrote, "[Her death was a] relief to me and yet traumatic in that it triggered depression, memories and pain." And a different survey respondent said, "Mom had to die before I could remember it." (1997, p. 233)

144

I never felt safe at home. Even when mother and I lived at my grandfather's, I knew that she was in charge of me and free to do anything she wanted. Mine was not a loving, safe family; I was left with a lifetime void. In therapy, I would return again and again to that deep sense of loss. My anguish was not so much for the child who was sexually violated but for the little girl who was neither loved nor protected.

Victims must come to see themselves as worthy of love and respect. Through no fault of their own, they received neither at home. In addressing this profound loss during therapy, identifying and building on the victims' other relationships is critical. Who genuinely cares about them? What good qualities do others see in them? Victims may have difficulty acknowledging that they have *any* strengths of character. When they perceive themselves as damaged goods—as a part of their contaminated family—they must be helped by the counselor-therapist to make that *fundamental psychological separation from their abuser(s)*.

In working with adolescents who experienced constant rejection from their parents, I would often say, "Tell me about some other adults who *do* seem to like you." If nobody quickly came to mind, we'd explore the possibilities together—teachers, coaches, youth leaders at church, neighbors, friends' parents, bosses at work—and eventually discover someone. "What do they do that makes you think they like you?" I'd ask. "What words would they use to describe you?" A powerful question because they had to come up with some positive qualities about themselves.

3) *The stigma of same-sex molestation.* As they work toward recovery, female victims of maternal incest may struggle with the added shame of female-female sexual behavior. Over the years, I became acutely aware of this unique aspect of mother-daughter incest. Although the same-sex factor never registered with me, it certainly did with some of the people I told about my abuse.

Myth: I had made love with another woman.

Fact: My mother had forced sexual behavior on me.

The myth implies mutual consent within a relationship between equals. The fact states that I was a powerless and unwilling victim. The distinction is important, not unlike the difference between making love and being raped.

More significant was my focus on the fact that my perpetrator was my *mother*—with the emphasis on her maternal relationship to me—rather than the fact my molester was female. My abuse stemmed not from my mother's sexual orientation; it was about power and control and manipulation. I never had any sexual-orientation confusion or questions; I was always strictly heterosexual. Except for Jeff, my empathetic second husband, all of my closest friends and supporters have always been women—my sisters of the heart. Thank God my mother's victimization of me did not destroy my ability to trust other women.

Sexual abuse affects the victim's body image, feelings about her gender, her sexuality and intimate relationships. My shameful feelings about my body came from my not measuring up to mother's lifelong definitions of feminine beauty and also from her on-going disregard for my privacy. Long before I would remember the overt sexual acts that she had performed on me, I had hated my body. She was average in height, but over-weight and disproportionately huge-busted; I was short, trim and, compared to her, I had no bosom. While I could celebrate how different I was from her in personality and character, I had—along the way—accepted her standards for physical beauty. Lacking in blonde hair and big breasts, I perceived myself as unfeminine and physically malformed. And after years of mother reprimanding me about poor posture, at age seventeen, I was finally diagnosed with severe scoliosis—curvature of the spine. The diagnosis did little to enhance my body image.

December 1972, just after Christmas, I flew home to Oregon with our new baby—to introduce her to my parents and grandfather. As I arrived at their house and took off my coat, my mother stared at my chest. "Oh my gosh, just look at you!" she shrieked. "Even having a second kid didn't do anything for your bust—you're still flat as a board!"

146

4) **Re-victimization.** Victims of child sexual abuse are sometimes re-victimized sexually by other people during their childhoods, adolescence or adulthoods (sexual assault, rape, domestic violence). In Rosencrans' 1997 research, "Approximately 70% of the daughters reported that *someone in addition to their mothers* sexually abused them." (p. 96)

Re-victimization—other people taking advantage of the victim or treating her unfairly—occurs in many different forms. In adulthood, female incest victims may be particularly vulnerable to sexual harassment on the job because of their inability to establish clear boundaries. Lacking self-confidence, they find it impossible to assert themselves with an authority figure, such as their boss. Sometimes they don't accurately "read" situations and people—they don't know which people to trust and which to avoid. Some resort to self-imposed social isolation to remain safe; others remain extremely naïve, trusting blindly in other people. Women may choose men who appear safe, only to be physically abused or to have their children later molested by these men.

I was one of the more fortunate victims—I was never assaulted by anyone other than my mother. I was never raped or physically injured but, as with many victims, I minimized some of the psychologically abusive experiences that happened to me.

During a mandatory visit home to Oregon in the mid-1970's, my mother had arranged for me to meet with one of my retired former high school teachers. He and his wife were social acquaintances of my mother. I had no desire to see him but I did not know how to get out of it without upsetting my mother so I acquiesced. Leaving my kids and husband at my parents' home, I drove to the teacher's house as planned. I thought he and his wife would both be home that afternoon. His wife wasn't. I thought it would feel comfortable. It didn't. I tried to steer the conversation to education issues—talking about my children and the schools in the Midwest. He kept the subject matter personal and the tone intimate. "You've grown into such a beautiful young woman," he commented, touching my arm. "I always thought you were special, Julie."

I made polite ("Always be polite, Missy!") excuses to leave

early. He walked me to my car and just when I thought I was safely behind the wheel, he suddenly leaned in the window, held my head firmly between his hands and French-kissed me. Stunned, I started the engine. He murmured goodbyes and something about maybe seeing me again. In a blur, I drove to my parents' house.

Overcome with disgust, in my head I screamed, "You dirty old man!" I had not done anything to encourage his behavior. Why did he do it? What was he thinking? Wanting understanding and support from another female, I made the mistake of telling my mother what had happened. She said that she didn't believe me—that I was making it up. "And, if it did happen," she added, "You asked for it."

Some victims worry about hurting the other person's feelings or embarrassing them. Or maybe we aren't that altruistic—maybe we are more concerned with just keeping the other person happy so they don't hurt us. I wanted to telephone my former teacher and confront him. "You took advantage of me this afternoon," I imagined telling him, calmly. "You had no right to grab and kiss me like that. I want an apology." I was not intimidated by anything he might say but I *was* still afraid of upsetting my mother. She was no longer a physical threat. So what could she have done to hurt me at that point in my life? She could have created a scene—denouncing me as "still a crazy whore" in front of my husband and two young children—with my father's backing, of course.

In the spring of 1981, as a thirty-three-year-old post-graduate student, I was student teaching at a local Midwest high school. My supervisor was the head of the department, married, in his fifties, well-known and highly regarded in the community. He seemed to respect my abilities and maturity, often leaving me alone, totally in charge of the classes. A clever man, he was totally professional and appropriate with me—up until the last few weeks of my internship. He knew that I needed to satisfactorily complete my student teaching to gain school counselor certification—he knew that I would stay and tough it out.

It all started on "Hawaiian Day"—part of the student body's special Spring activities week. I was grading papers at a table in the department work area before the school day started. He came up behind me, put a cellophane "Hawaiian lei" over my head, placed both of his hands on my cheeks and thrust his tongue in my mouth. I was shocked and repulsed. After that morning, he found every possible opportunity to be close to me. Stroking my arm, leaning over me when I was working, making sexual comments and jokes, asking me to go have drinks with him. I felt powerless. I thought I had no choice but to tolerate his behavior if I were to obtain my certificate and hopefully, a counseling position for that Fall. He had the power to pass or fail my student teaching; he would write my final evaluation and letter of endorsement. Without an enthusiastic recommendation from him, I would not even be able to get an interview. He knew it, and so did I.

Why didn't I file a grievance—sue him for harassment? Sexual harassment laws, regulations and complaint procedures were still being developed and tested back then:

"In August 1981, the U.S. Department of Education reaffirmed its jurisdiction over sexual harassment complaints. Therefore, sexual harassment in educational institutions is against the law and is enforced by the U.S. Department of Education, Office for Civil Rights. Although sexual harassment of students is emphasized as being a violation of Title IX, employees of educational programs and activities which receive federal funds are also protected from sexual harassment under Title IX." (U. S. Department of Education, Office for Civil Rights)

One afternoon at school I found another student teacher sitting on the floor in the women's bathroom, crying. She was having almost identical problems with her supervisor. I was furious for her. We drove to the university and together we reported their behavior to the Education Department. But if we quit our student-teaching assignments right then, we were the ones who would suffer; we'd have to repeat our internships in the Fall and would not be employable until the following year. We insisted on staying but we wanted a record of their on-going harassment in case either man tried to give us an unwarranted, poor, final evaluation.

We developed strategies for the two of us to get through those last weeks—staying together at lunch, seeking each other out after classes so we would not be alone with our supervisors. With our final teaching evaluations safely in hand, we made a last, albeit informal, complaint to the university. We were told that a new statement describing sexual harassment and grievance procedures would be placed in the handbooks given to all student teachers. We hoped that our reporting would make a difference for others.

Do sexual-abuse victims make easy targets later in life? Courtois (1988) noted the following:

> Studies of women involved in antisocial and deviant behavior (e.g., prostitution, drug abuse, delinquent and criminal behavior, involvement with criminals) and studies of inpatient, outpatient deinstitutionalized, and chronically victimized populations are remarkably consistent in the finding that a high percentage have experienced childhood sexual abuse. Incest can definitely be a factor in the development of antisocial behavior and of self-destructive and revictimizing behavior. (p. 114)

Yet other female victims live inconspicuous lives, working and raising their families, only occasionally and very privately, falling apart. That described me. "In contrast to survivors with impaired functioning, some women function quite well. They extend the childhood pattern of successful school functioning to their social, occupational, and familial functioning as adults." (Courtois, p.114)

Courtois continued,

> Even though these women are successful when assessed on a number of criteria, many describe themselves as feeling disconnected from their skills and accomplishments and as impostors waiting to be found out. These "superwomen" types are susceptible to burnout and other stress-related maladies due to the self-neglect that usually accompanies their overfunctioning. (p. 114)

150

In therapy, I also discovered how controlled my childhood had been and how restricted my internal world still felt. Outside of my roles of mother and school counselor, I wasn't clear who I was or who I could be. Victims who had little power or voice in childhood, may become compliant, deferential and non-confrontational employees and spouses—unconscious martyrs—who often don't ask for much in life. If a teacher repeatedly volunteers for extra duties, she can't blame the principal for allowing her to do them. If a husband asks, "Where would you like to go for dinner?" and his wife responds with "Oh, I don't care, you choose," she can hardly complain that her vote never counted. I never had much practice making decisions when I was growing up. On a variety of topics, I didn't have an opinion—I didn't even know what I liked or disliked.

Therapy was eye opening. I was not aware that my ex and I had such different outlooks and preferences or how I'd acquiesced on many personal decisions. I loved getting together with other people; my ex-husband did not. During the last six years of our marriage, not counting relatives, we had guests to our home on just five occasions. Numerous times he would tell me, after the fact, that we had been invited to someone's home or to a party but he "got us out of it."

I completed my therapy in October 1988. In October 1989, I left the marriage. My son was 20, my daughter, 17. My ex-husband was and is a wonderful father.

5) *Breaking the cycle of abuse*. I have never abused my children or any other children. That fact gave me peace of mind at times when nothing else could soothe my psychological pain. I took comfort in knowing that even if I felt "different" or "crazy," I never harmed my kids. After I fully recalled the abuse, I praised myself (and thanked God) that somehow I had always been safe with my kids. The pattern was changed; the cycle of abuse was broken.

But that was not enough. Like many victims, unaware and still in denial, I did not immediately see the danger signs when my mother was around my children. I shudder to think what might have happened had we lived closer. What if we had lived in the same town? What if she had babysat for them, frequently?

Victims of maternal incest may fear "Will I be like my mother?" and "Will I abuse my own children?" We also need to ask, "Will I recognize sexual abuse when it is happening right smack in front of me?" Why should we believe that a mother who perpetrates her own daughter or son would magically leave her grandchildren alone? The grandchildren are not safe! Protecting grandchildren (and other children) from the perpetrator needs to be a priority.

The problem, of course, is that victims of mother-daughter incest often don't remember their abuse until later in their adult lives. By adulthood, they may have children of their own and have already handed them over to their perpetrators for cross-generational victimization.

When we explored this subject in therapy, I still minimized my son's experience with my mother. I had talked with my children over the years about privacy and inappropriate touch and to always tell, even if the adult making them uncomfortable was a close friend or relative—even a parent. When they were young I had said, "If I ever say or do something that makes you feel embarrassed or uncomfortable, I want you to tell your Dad." I added, "And if your Dad says or does something that doesn't feel quite right, he would want you to tell me. That's how we keep you feeling comfortable and safe." The only time my mother tried anything sexual with my kids was that one Christmas. That was more than enough.

I encouraged my kids to think independently and to question what others told them. I consciously let them make as many of their own decisions as possible. Two-year-olds should be able to choose which shirts and pants and socks they want to wear. I well remember many non-color-coordinated creative combinations. *They* thought they looked awesome. That's how they learn to make choices—through a lot of daily practice. It's empowering and fun and something I hardly ever experienced growing up.

Adult victims need *to tell their children about their fundamental psychological separation from their abuser(s).* The differences in character between the adult victim and the maternal perpetrator need to be labeled and discussed for their own kids' psychological well-being. If the adult incest victim has terminated the relationship with her or his mother, the reasons need to be shared with the children at an appropriate age. If the relationship continues and we act as though the offending parent is a decent human being, how can we admonish our kids not to spend too much time with grandma? We send conflicting messages that will puzzle but not protect.

This was particularly difficult for me. I had not yet remembered the earliest abuse but I *always* remembered fourth grade and beyond. I knew that my mother was creepy and disrespectful and frightening long before I was ever able to characterize her as a "perpetrator."

She was the reason we had an attorney draw up our wills—planning what would happen with our children if we should both die. When I declared I wanted an airtight will that my parents could never challenge, the lawyer appeared surprised. I said my mother would definitely try to get custody of my kids and I would rather have them become wards of the state than be raised by her. I may not have recalled the earliest sexual abuse but I *knew* my mother was dangerous to children. We established a contingency order of five or six other relatives and friends who would have gladly raised the children. We spelled it out, in no uncertain terms, that my parents were never to gain custody.

One summer, when my children were thirteen and ten, we took an extended family car trip West to visit Disneyland, Las Vegas, and both sets of grandparents. My parents took all of us to a mountain resort for a few days. In spite of my mother's attempts to control our daily schedules with prescribed meal times and rest breaks, we had fun riding horses, swimming and biking. While I could never stand up for myself with her, I could challenge her on the behalf of my kids. No, my ten-year-old daughter did not need any nap—she wanted to go horseback riding with me.

My son and I were talking during this visit when unexpectedly he said, "Mom, I don't think Grandma likes me." I looked him in the eye and said, "You're absolutely right!" It surprised him. I continued, "She can't stand you, honey, because you are a really kind person and you treat people well, and she isn't like that." Hugging him, I whispered, "I think I'd worry if she liked you. By the way, just so you know, she doesn't like me either!"

Fear: Female victims of maternal incest are afraid that they, too, will abuse children—that it is somehow learned, ingrained behavior.

Fact: Most female victims of maternal incest do not sexually abuse others.

Studies of female incest victims (with either male or female perpetrators) do not support a pattern of the female victims becoming perpetrators. Female victims seem to be more at risk for becoming workaholic counselors, teachers, social workers and volunteers than child molesters.

In Finkelhor's 1994 article, "Current Information on the Scope and Nature of Child Sexual Abuse," on page 47 the author cited various research findings regarding the impact of sexual abuse on boys as compared to girls:

> The clinical literature observes that boys are more likely than girls to act out in aggressive and antisocial ways as a result of abuse. [65] (Bolton, Morris, and MacEachron, 1989)

> Boys are also seen as having more concerns about gender role and sexual orientation because both victimization in general and homosexual victimization in particular are so stigmatizing to males. [66] (Urquiza, 1988)

> Although these observations may be accurate, outcome studies have actually had difficulty demonstrating consistent differences in symptomatology between abused boys and girls or men and women. [67] (Finkelhor, 1990)

> It would appear, based on current research, that there are more similarities than differences in the impact of abuse. One notable exception concerns the apparent greater likelihood that men who were sexually abused as children will express some sexual interest in children. [66, 68] (Urquiza, 1988; Bagley, Wood, and Young, 1994)

This does seem to confirm another clinical perception that abused boys, more often than girls, are at increased risk to become perpetrators. (p. 47)

What might account for some of the differences in how boys and girls respond to their sexual abuse? Two possible factors come to mind. First, from my experience counseling middle-school and high-school boys, they hated being identified as "victims." Whether it was psychological bullying from their peers or physical blows from their stepdads, boys were deeply ashamed of having been victimized by anyone. Anger would often mask their pain. Feelings of vulnerability and hurt were stuffed. Often they allowed no sad feelings for themselves and no empathy for other victims. Rage was turned outward and many times led to a pattern of antisocial behavior—sexual harassment toward other students, fighting, truancy, suspensions or expulsion, vandalism, theft, drug use and sales, assault. When these kids were charismatic, attractive and bright, they were sometimes leaders of their own small peer groups, keeping the others in line with fear and intimidation. I saw this pattern with both boys and girls, but more often with boys.

In contrast, a second victim-response pattern I observed was to turn the anger and pain inward, targeting themselves. Cutting and other forms of self-mutilation, depression, suicidal ideation and/or attempts, promiscuity and self-imposed isolation were common. Sorrowful and shamed-based, they were at risk for self-destruction. The idea of mistreating another person was unfathomable to them; they deeply empathized with other kids with problems and with other victims of abuse. Open, trusting and vulnerable, they were often the targets of the victims-turned-bullies. While some boys demonstrated these behaviors, more often I saw this pattern with girls.

Victims (more often boys) who acted out against other people received punishments, consequences and court sentences. Victims (more often girls) who targeted only themselves received support, compassion and counseling.

Second, boys receive mixed messages about the appropriateness of sexual activities between adult females and adolescent or pubescent boys. From film and television, from a litany of sexual jokes and stories, boys may come to conclude that sex between older women and under-age boys is acceptable behavior. Boys who are victimized by their mothers, or by other adult females, may be led to think that adult-child sex is not that bad for a kid. If they remain unaware and they deny the harm in such activities, they may themselves become perpetrators.

6) *Resolution—from "victim" to "survivor!"* I have intentionally used the term "victim" throughout this chapter. I believe there to be a crucial difference between being a victim and becoming a survivor. *A survivor must demonstrate both empathy and awareness.* Feeling empathy for children ultimately prevents a victim from becoming a perpetrator herself. But the awareness of sexually abusive behavior will help to keep her children safe from molestation by others. Both qualities are necessary to become a survivor.

Any woman who was incested in childhood but who then perpetrates against a child remains a *victim*—re-enacting her own abuse. A *survivor*, in contrast, is healthy and safe with kids. Survivors don't sexually abuse other human beings.

I always had empathy. I would rather have died than perpetrated against a child. But without information about the dynamics of mother-daughter sexual abuse and with the repression of my own early incest experiences, I lacked awareness. In spite of my clear, unrepressed memories of mother's bizarre behavior during my adolescence, it never occurred to me that she might perpetrate my children. Her conduct toward me during my teenage years should have signaled the likelihood of overt sexual abuse in early childhood. Yet, I was unaware. Being unaware of the dynamics of mother-child sexual abuse, like many others, I was still a victim when I entered therapy. Six months later, I emerged an enlightened, resilient survivor.

Victims' timely recollections of abuse and their commitment to therapy are not sufficient to keep children safe. If we are serious about fighting child sexual abuse, we need to be pro-active. Just as we now talk about father-daughter incest, we must teach children and parents and counselors about the continuum of maternal sexual abuse behaviors. Empathy alone is not enough. If awareness is lacking, our children are at risk.

Chapter 9

Beyond Survival

WAS MY MOTHER A VICTIM?

It doesn't matter.

Close women friends as well as attendees at my conference workshops have asked, "Do you think your mother was molested when *she* was a little girl?" At first, I was stunned by their inquiry. I imagined it as somehow trying to justify my mother's abusive behavior toward me. Now I understand they ask it in a sincere attempt to make sense out of the unthinkable.

Nevertheless, my response has always been the same: "It's irrelevant."

I have no evidence to indicate whether my mother was sexually abused during her childhood. She maintained that she always had close relationships with both of her parents. Had she been molested, I would still have no sympathy for her because when she repeatedly and intentionally abused me, *she knew it was wrong.* She consistently labeled her incest with me as secretive, and she threatened to harm me if I told anybody. When parents threaten to maim their children if they tell anyone their secrets, parents *know* they are doing wrong.

My mother knew it was wrong and I believe, given the opportunity, she would have molested both of my children. She was "grooming" my young son during that Christmas visit—seeing what she could get away with and how he might react.

Having suffered childhood sexual abuse is no excuse for perpetuating the cycle. If victims don't do the therapeutic work it takes to become survivors, future generations have little hope of living healthy, productive lives.

GUILT AND THE ONLY CHILD

Another often-asked question is, "Why didn't you just end the relationship with your parents after you left home? Or after your marriage? Or, for Pete's sake, at least stop visiting your father after your mother died?"

It is difficult to explain to people who grew up in healthy families. I was a "good victim." Victims learn to do self-blame, shame and guilt so well. It had become as automatic as breathing. Add in the "only-child guilt syndrome" and I felt that I had no options but to stay in the relationship with them.

Since childhood, I was forced to be compliant and respectful to my parents out of perceived penalty of rejection, abandonment, or physical harm. Those were strong deterrents. It was almost impossible for me to confront them or stand up to them ever on my own behalf.

Whenever I looked at myself through their eyes, I was overcome with shame and humiliation. My parents had but one child and I turned out to be "a crazy whore" who got pregnant, moved far away, worked in the schools and was nothing to boast about at bridge club. I reasoned the least I could do was keep the relationship going and send them letters and photos so they could brag about their grandchildren. I could not have survived every-Sunday family dinners at their house if we had stayed in the same town. Living far away in the Midwest meant that relatively little was asked of me.

On the phone every Sunday, I was reminded of my crimes and mistakes and my deservedly bleak future. When I stayed home as a full-time mom, mother would tell me how my Ph.D. husband would outgrow me and surely leave me for a more well-educated (and undoubtedly more well-endowed) colleague. After I enrolled in graduate school, she chastised me for neglecting my duties as a mother and declared that my children would certainly suffer for it. I couldn't win. Regularly I'd hang up the phone and burst into tears.

I would not have willfully hurt anybody—including my parents—and I know that my ending the relationship would have upset them greatly. Plus, for years I was in denial and unaware of the totality of the abuse. Having minimized and downplayed her inappropriate behavior throughout my fourth- through twelfth-grade years, I did not feel justified in suddenly severing the relationship. I'd regarded her intimate mother-daughter activities with me as "bizarre" and "weird" but not as sexually exploitative. Incidents of early abuse stayed repressed until after she died. Even after she cornered my son Christmas 1977, I would not then have described her as a sexual abuse perpetrator.

After my mother died, I felt sorry for my father. He was alone. I was the only immediate family he had. Most of the time he sounded contented playing golf, attending activities with his military organizations and fraternal clubs and going to the country club with several lady friends. But once a year, I would think that I *had* to go see him, even if it took a heavy emotional toll. It did not seem too much for a parent to ask. Plus, if I didn't, there would be hell to pay with criticism and guilt. "Too selfish to even come see your old man, huh?" he asked, one year when I had said I would not be able to visit that summer. "Yep, that's you, all right," he added. "Always just thinking of yourself, aren't you?" I folded. I went.

After therapy, when I *knew* what mother had done to me, I still visited him. Now I carried my survivor tools with me: the notepad and tally-mark comment sheets, a list of chores and activities to keep us occupied, a directory of mutual acquaintances and relatives that we could visit and a psychological shield to deflect the verbal assaults he predictably would launch. I chose to go because it was easier on me than ending the relationship would have been. At least that is what I told myself each time I planned another trip home.

160

FLASHBACK

I have not been in therapy since 1988 (except for five free employee assistance sessions with a counselor when I separated from my husband). I have taken anti-depressant medication twice in my life: when I was going through the divorce in 1989 and for about four months a few years before my father's death.

Flashbacks hit me only occasionally. The last one was in December 2004. We had a young child visiting in our home—an innocent little dark-haired five-year-old girl—sweet and trusting. After she left, I suddenly flashed back to when I was around her age. I sat in the recliner in our living room, rocking, scrunching my shoulders, my arms folded tightly across my chest. I was the wee child again—scared, trapped, panicked and so overwhelmingly sad. Tears flowed. I could not move. So fragile that I thought I would break if anyone touched me; so totally alone. Paralyzed with fear, I could hear my mother's voice and sense her dreaded touch.

My husband stayed in the room with me. He said it was horrible for him to watch. It took about an hour for it to pass and for me to fully recover. Emotionally and physically exhausted, I went to bed. The question I kept asking then and always will is "Why?" Knowing the psychological and analytical reasons for her behavior will never silence the small voice inside that asks, "But, Mother, how could you?"

TRYING TO MAKE SENSE OUT OF THE INCONCEIVABLE

In *Child Sexual Abuse: New Theory and Research* (1984), Finkelhor offered the "Four-Preconditions Model of Sexual Abuse" to describe the pre-conditions necessary in order for sexual abuse to occur. These remain highly applicable to discussions of mother-daughter and mother-son incest today:

1. A potential offender needed to have some motivation to abuse a child sexually.

2. The potential offender had to overcome internal inhibitions against acting on that motivation.

3. The potential offender had to overcome external impediments to committing sexual abuse.

4. The potential offender or some other factor had to undermine or overcome a child's possible resistance to the sexual abuse. (p. 54)

Finkelhor identified several factors that may impact the motivation (pre-condition number one) to sexually abuse but not all three have to be present for sexual abuse to take place. These included: emotional congruence, sexual arousal and blockage. (pp. 54-55) My mother's emotional need to feel powerful and in control while simultaneously seeking nurturing may have contributed to her incentive to abuse me. She controlled our sexual interactions to meet her needs and to connect with me, but on her terms. She sexualized the emotional closeness of the normal mother-child relationship. Also, she *was* "blocked" from any regular marital sexual relations when my father was stationed overseas. Perhaps she saw the closeness she thrust on me as justified by my father's absence.

Pursuing the model further, I *could* theorize that my mother overcame any ***internal inhibitions*** (pre-condition number two) against mother-child incest because she had been molested during her own childhood. But I have no other reason for believing that she was ever victimized. I also don't think the other variables for overcoming inhibitions—alcohol, psychosis, senility and impulse disorder—cited in the model applied to my mother. (pp. 55-58)

So what role did my mother's narcissism play? Her lack of empathy—her inability to understand and to identify with my emotional needs—may have played a key role in overriding her inhibitions against sexual abuse. She experienced an unexpected, difficult, unwanted pregnancy and traumatic, life-threatening childbirth. Then weeks of her ill health coupled with my isolation from her in a hospital incubator may have totally undermined any attachment bond. It may be far easier to molest someone whom you view as a "thing" as opposed to viewing as your child.

Finkelhor also refers to overcoming ***external impediments*** (pre-condition number three)—factors about the home environment that make it difficult for the pre-disposed parent to molest. Consider how much easier it is for the abuser when the non-offending parent is absent (due to illness, travel, work, divorce), or does not protect the child (because of a lack of awareness, apathy, chemical dependency) and/or the family is socially isolated. (pp. 54-60) My father being stationed overseas on military assignments and then routinely abdicating most parenting responsibilities even when he was home, made it easier for my mother to abuse me.

"Impediments," are good. We *want* potential sexual perpetrators to be impeded! If external impediments are in place, the pre-disposed abuser can't as easily molest. Therefore, we want both of the parents aware of potentially abusive behaviors and watching each other's interactions with the children. I submit that high-quality parent-education classes, peer-support groups, home visitations and individual counseling services can actually *be* impediments to child abuse.

We need to address the subject of child abuse—physical, emotional, sexual and neglect—in all pre-natal parenting classes. Using surveys and interviews, we can help expectant parents explore their own abuse histories. If we can't or won't talk about child abuse, including child sexual abuse, how can we hope to break the cycle? We need to educate parents about what constitutes sexual abuse, how to recognize the warning signs and how to intervene to protect their children, even when the suspected offender is a family member. Guest speakers, activities, group discussion and home visitors can focus on different parenting styles, appropriate forms of discipline and healthy parent-child boundaries. Both individual and couples counseling should be available for participants upon request.

"Healthy Families America," is one promising research-based national model offering education, home visits and referrals for expectant and new parents. To date, "Healthy Families America" exists in over 450 communities in the United States and Canada.

Participation is voluntary but ninety percent of the families invited to participate in the program have accepted services. (Healthy Families America web site)

Can pre-natal and parenting classes offer information and experiential activities that will reinforce mother-child bonding? Can we enhance new mothers' ability to empathize with their children as a way to prevent mother-child incest? In an article entitled *"Promoting Attachment in Adopted Infants,"* (January 2006), author Jessica Jerard offers new adoptive mothers specific behavioral recommendations for increasing mother-child attachment. ("Families With Children from China" web site)

She describes explicit feeding, holding and interactive activities that can strengthen the mutual mother-infant bond. If these skills can be taught to new adoptive mothers, why can't they be used with new biological mothers? And why do we presume that all biological mothers instinctively empathize with and attach to their infants? Mine certainly didn't.

But according to Finkelhor's model, "all four preconditions have to be fulfilled for the abuse to occur." (p. 62) Along with adult education-prevention programs, we may be able to intervene by addressing the factors that influence a child's possible resistance to the sexual abuse (pre-condition number four). Dynamics cited as potentially aiding the perpetrator in overcoming the child's resistance to sexual behaviors include whether the child: is emotionally secure, knowledgeable about sexual abuse, is coerced and has a trusting relationship with the abuser. (pp. 54-62) Mothers who incest their daughters or sons exercise extreme control over their parent-child relationships; they have gained their children's dependence through coercion. *Of the four factors critical to the child's ability to resist the perpetrator, the only factor we may be able to directly impact is the child's awareness of sexual abuse.*

We need to examine how and what we are teaching children about sexual abuse. It is important to identify women as well as men—mothers and stepmothers in addition to fathers and stepfathers—as potential perpetrators in all child-abuse literature and materials and prevention programs. We must be certain not to exclude females—family friends, neighbors, sisters, aunties and grandmas. One simple and effective change is to use "his or her" instead of only the male personal pronoun when talking about someone who might hurt a child.

Teachers, counselors and other school professionals who present the school programs on child sexual abuse must be both knowledgeable about the subject and genuinely comfortable talking about it with kids. If the presenters convey revulsion by their scrunched shoulders and facial grimaces, they could unwittingly silence victims for years. Adults have to be able to handle kids' sometimes difficult questions about a subject that is awkward, frightening and embarrassing to them.

Receptive adult follow-up is critical. The presenters should be members of the school staff—trusted, known adults who will still be accessible three weeks later when a child may decide to disclose. Too often these programs are "one-time shots" with a local expert, who is a stranger to the children and unavailable for follow-up.

To prevent incest, we work primarily with the adults; to intervene early when incest occurs, we work primarily with the children. Both adults and children need to know that a mother's touch can be devastating.

THE "D" WORD

Decades have passed since my mother molested me. And it's been over four years now since my father died. Jeff and I met in 1990 and were married in 1994. I told him all of my ugly secrets and he did not run away. Jeff did more than just stay. He held me and let me weep. For the first time in my life I felt safe.

All childhood abuse—whether primarily physical, emotional or sexual—leaves scars. Wounds to the outside of our bodies heal far more quickly than those to our souls. Throughout our lives, survivors of child abuse struggle with the "D" word: "D" is for *deserve*. Sometimes, even now, I expect my happy, fulfilling life to be yanked away and the gods to mockingly ask, "What made you think *you* deserved to be so loved?"

Parents who abuse their children are different from the parents who don't. Sounds obvious but we forget sometimes. The family dynamics are different—they have to be in order for the abuse to occur. Some people might presume the family to be sane and normal twenty-three and one-half hours a day—then the dad suddenly rages out and physically abuses his kids—and then family life is somehow sane and normal again. Or, as in my case, they might think that our relationships were healthy and safe—then for fifteen minutes at nap time my mother would molest me—but then it would be healthy and safe again. It wasn't.

A "cycle of violence" exists within the family, yes. Children experience abusive episodes; they rebound in the aftermath; then they wait for the next time. But even though the family might appear "normal" to the outside world in between the episodes of abuse, it is NOT. The children are *always on guard*—watching and waiting for the angry fist, or, in my case, the too-gentle touch. They live with fear and anxiety as they try to make sense out of their parents' behavior and to anticipate what will happen next. This incessant apprehension is not natural. I submit that families in which child abuse occurs do not ever genuinely experience emotional normalcy. All they have are lulls before the next storms. Not normal.

The emotional abuse that accompanies all physical and sexual abuse includes this relentless anxiety, or as my elementary school teachers labeled it—"nervousness." During the earlier incidents of molestation and those of covert abuse as a teenager, my mother was sugary-nice to me; the rest of the time she was critical, distant and judgmental. Neither set of behaviors was natural or healthy. What messages did they give me about my self worth in the eyes of my own mother?

Of course my childhood abuse still affects me, but in smaller ways over time. Today my thoughts might be disrupted for a while but my life is not. In fact, my parents' personalities and character and my mother's bizarre behaviors come to mind far more often than any explicit earlier sexual experiences with her.

Some of the side effects of my mother-daughter incest include:

1) *Shame*. Much of my life was shame-based. The secret sexual indignities she forced on me were humiliating. It was difficult to forgive myself for allowing the bizarre intimacy (exhibitionism, voyeurism) to continue throughout my high-school years.

I am profoundly ashamed—but now it is *not* for having been molested. As a survivor, I know it was not my fault. I also know that I never abused my own children. I am ashamed of my parents—of who my parents were and for how they treated not just me, but other people, too.

After mother died, I tried to atone for some of the wrongs she had done. I gave my uncle the monogrammed sterling silverware she had hoarded over the years. It bore the initial of her maiden name—my uncle's last name—the name my mother had not used since her marriage in 1946. The silverware was concealed in a box in the basement. Why had she kept it? I believe she had held onto it just so her brother could not have it. When my father died in 2002, I was able to finally return old photos and cherished family heirlooms to her brother. My father had stockpiled these items for the nineteen years following mother's death. In his mind, he felt somehow entitled to them.

I also started monthly contributions to the Southern Poverty Law Center, a civil rights organization dedicated to fighting racism, intolerance and crimes of hate. My support of the center continues; it helps me to feel like I am making some amends.

2) *Extreme self-criticism*. Sometimes when I make a simple mistake, I repeat my parents' old put-downs. "You stupid idiot," I say to myself for not remembering to buy a needed item at the grocery store. Secretly swearing and muttering the foulest of names, I know instantly the negative self-talk is neither logical nor merited. Just more residue from the lifelong emotional abuse.

3) *Hypersensitivity to victimization*. My sense of humor is restricted. I can't stand practical jokes. I over-empathize with the person who is fooled. I worry about their feelings; I don't want to see

them hurt or confused or ridiculed. When my husband and I watch "Candid Camera" reruns or similar programs, I need to know that the targeted person is all right at the end of the show. My mother duped me; I was the ultimate fool for believing her lies. I never want to be fooled—intentionally mislead or betrayed—again and I don't enjoy watching someone else be the victim of a prank or practical joke.

I've discovered I lack a "normal" sense of humor about sexual matters, too. I overreact occasionally to jokes and e-mails from friends and family—deleting them in disgust. My responses are often irrational.

Sometimes I am hyper vigilant for sexual exploitation, even when it probably doesn't exist. I tend to see victims everywhere. For example, "Playboy" magazine centerfold models *choose* to be on display, naked. (They are not secretly photographed through a peephole. They are not nine years old.) Yet, any female nudity in the media often stirs up overwhelming feelings of sadness for me. I can also easily become upset about the use of sex and exploitation of girls and women in advertising.

4) *Triggers.* Everyone has memory triggers—the smell of pipe tobacco reminds someone of their beloved grandfather or the aroma of an apple pie takes another person back to their auntie's sunny kitchen. Survivors of incest may involuntarily respond to an array of triggers that immediately take them back to their childhood abuse.

Incidents in my daily life can trigger memories of my mother and of specific acts of sexual abuse. Knives, dirty jokes, hearing other women speak lovingly about their mothers, television programs about child abuse, someone sneaking up on me (my startle response is extreme), bold-red lipsticks, references to Bette Davis, certain mannerisms like pursing one's lips, Q-tips and old Doris Day songs like "Que Sera Sera" are some common triggers for me. My reactions seemingly come out of nowhere. My husband watches. He will observe me shudder or flinch or curl my toes or just silently check out for a few seconds. I bounce back quickly because I've had a lot of practice. Occasionally, he will ask, "Are you OK?" His asking helps to make me so.

~~~

And now? As I publicly disclose my history of abuse, I peel away layers of shame with each re-telling. Soon, I think, there will be very little shame left. Soon, I will tell my story without my voice cracking even once. It is not *my* dishonor. *All shame belongs to my parents*—the abuser and her silent partner.

I am a privileged survivor. Truly. Gifts of dissociation, resiliency, motherhood, friendship, work, love, faith, therapy, humor, passion and peace have all been mine. Throughout my life, I was fortunate to cross paths with many people who cared for me. And I believe that has made all the difference.

Mother-child sexual abuse is a "yucky" subject. It makes people uncomfortable. They don't want to hear about it. And because it is more unusual, more bizarre, more hidden and perhaps *the* most taboo subject, mother-daughter incest is the very last form of sexual abuse that anyone wants to consider.

~~~

For years I kept quiet. I break my silence now on behalf of the children who at this moment are being sexually abused by their mothers, on behalf of adult victims who have not yet told anyone and on behalf of the next generation, that they might not be harmed by their mothers' touch.

Appendix A

ELEMENTARY SCHOOL REPORT CARDS:

Julie's elementary-school report cards; teachers' comments and parents' responses

San Diego County Schools
REPORT TO PARENTS
Kindergarten
195 2 - 1953

Pupil's Name _____ Julie Taylor _____

School ____ South Oceanside _____ Principal _O. R. Palmquist_

Dear Parents:

The first year of school is important for your child. We want him to be happy and successful so that he may develop new abilities and form habits which will make his future school years also happy and successful.

Different children cut their teeth at different ages, begin to walk and talk at different times, and learn at different rates. The abilities which our program tries to develop are listed on the back page. This is my report to you of your child's progress toward these goals. We do not expect all children to master these goals at any one time, but by the end of the school year, most of them will have done so. We hope this list will help you understand the kinds of experiences your child will have at school this year.

I shall be very glad to discuss this report with you. If you call or write for an appointment, we can have an uninterrupted time together. We believe that in addition to this semiannual written report there should be a minimum of two parent-teacher conferences during the school year.

Yours truly,

_____ Mrs. Crumley _____
Teacher

1st Reporting Period

Teacher's Comments

Julie is a fine little Kg. and I enjoy her very much. She is cooperative & well liked by her little classmates and most anxious to follow all directions. Gets upset easily tho, when she thinks things are not quite right, when I assure her that all is well she responds readily and is happy again. Is she sensitive at home too? Or perhapes because we are all still new to her at school?

_____   H Crumley
Date   Teacher's Signature

Parent's Comments

Mrs. Crumley -

Yes, Julie is very sensitive at home, but as you say, easily reassured if she thinks something is not quite right. She is in her glory when she is in large groups and really seems happy and confident most of the time. Her sensitivity shows itself too, in nightly dreams and frequent nightmares. If any problems to arise will be more than happy to co-operate in any way. Please feel free to call on us.

February 4, 1953   Mrs. Thomas G. Taylor
Date   Parent's Signature
                          Thomas G. Taylor

SAN DIEGO CITY SCHOOLS
San Diego, California

PRIMARY PUPIL GROWTH REPORT

WILL ANGIER
SCHOOL
Grantville

Message from the Superintendent

Dear Parent or Guardian:

The instructional program of the San Diego City Schools is planned to provide the best possible education for each child of our community. A carefully planned course of study serves as a guide for promoting continuous growth in the basic skills. The school is also concerned with the physical, social and emotional growth of the child. It seeks to help each boy and girl to develop to the best of his or her ability. The total school program provides opportunity for the student to develop as a well-adjusted, self-supporting, actively participating citizen.

Your child's progress report has been prepared in terms of his growth and development. It indicates:

. . . growth and progress in the basic skills.

. . . social and emotional growth and adjustment.

. . . areas of study where improvement is needed.

. . . ways that improvement can be achieved.

There will be three reports sent home during the school year.

You are invited to discuss your child's progress with his teacher or with the principal. By working together, the home and the school can better help each boy and girl make progress.

Sincerely yours,
R. C. Dallard
~~WILL C. CRAWFORD~~, Superintendent
San Diego City Schools

Pupil _Julia Ann Taylor_

Grade _One_ _Robert L. Cottam_ Principal

Form 30645

172

Teacher's Message

1st Report: **Parent's Reply** 👉

Julia is a very quite, good girl. She is sometimes a little nervous, but is doing good work.

Teacher _Dorothy Childers_ Date _11/23/53_

2nd Report:

Julia understands reading enough to do homework or enjoy library books. Her school work is satisfactory

Teacher _Dorothy Childers_ Date _1/29/54_

3rd Report: Julia is a very nice addition to our first grade. She has adjusted to our room easily and well. She does nice work. I suggest that Julia continue reading this summer by getting prepuners, primers, and first readers from the library.

Teacher _Mrs. M.E. Roche_ Date _May 6, 1954_

173

Parent's Reply

Your signature indicates that you have examined your child's report and discussed it with him. Since the home and school together have the responsibility for the guidance of your child, a report of your observations at home will be most helpful. We also welcome your reaction to your child's report and any suggestions you may have for more effectively helping your child.

Comments, Reactions, Suggestions

1st Report: *We're happy Julie is doing well. If there is anything we can do to help in her growth, let us know. We haven't noticed the nervousness but she is very sensitive and aware of others. She comes home with her woes, we explain the "why or wherefore" and she's happy again.*

Parent *Mrs. Thos. S. Taylor* Date *November 25, 1953*

2nd Report:

Parent *Mrs. Thos. S. Taylor* Date *February 7, 1954*

3rd Report: *We're glad to hear she is mixing well with the class, etc. She looks forward to every day at school and seems very happy. We'll see that she does summer reading and she's looking forward to a library trip. If we can help in any other way, please let us know.*

Parent *Mrs. Thos. S. Taylor* Date *May 17, 1954*

SAN DIEGO CITY SCHOOLS
San Diego, California

PRIMARY PUPIL GROWTH REPORT

Grantville
SCHOOL

Message from the Superintendent

Dear Parent or Guardian

The instructional program of the San Diego City Schools is planned to provide the best possible education for each child of our community. A carefully planned course of study serves as a guide for promoting continuous growth in the basic skills. The school is also concerned with the physical, emotional, and social growth of the child. It seeks to help each boy and girl to develop to the best of his or her ability and to become a well-adjusted, self-supporting, actively participating citizen.

Your child's progress report has been prepared in terms of his growth and development. It indicates:

... growth and progress in the basic skills.
... social growth and adjustment.
... areas of study where improvement is needed.
... ways that improvement can be achieved.

There will be three reports sent home during the school year.

You are invited to discuss your child's progress with his teacher or with the principal. By working together, the home and the school can better help each boy and girl make progress.

Sincerely yours,

RALPH DAILARD, Superintendent
San Diego City Schools

Pupil _Julia Ann Taylor_

Grade _2_ _____ Principal

Notice of Assignment

Grade placement for September 19___ Grade _3_ Room Number _4_

Mary Grace Ponder
Teacher's Signature

Stock No. 22-16-690

175

Teacher's Message

1st Report: **Parent's Reply** ☞

Having Julia is certainly a pleasure. She does very good and very neat work. I know you are justly proud of her. Stop by to see me anytime.

Teacher _M. G. Ponder_ Date _11-18-54_

2nd Report:

Julia is continuing her good work. She has a sweet personality and is very dependable. Sometimes I feel she gets very nervous if everything isn't just "perfect". Perhaps you can help her in reading— I believe she needs more confidence, also expression.

Teacher _M. G. Ponder,_ Date _2-3-1955_

3rd Report: Dear Mr. & Mrs. Taylor. Julia is an ideal little girl. She is so mature and dependable. Her progress has been very good, and I know how proud you are of her. She is loved by all in the class, and I have certainly enjoyed working with

Teacher _Mary Grace Ponder_ Date _5-5-55_

her this year. Julia — How proud I would be if my child brought home a report like this!! Mr. & Mrs.

176

Parent's Reply

Your signature indicates that you have examined your child's report and discussed it with him. Since the home and school together have the responsibility for the guidance of your child, a report of your observations at home will be most helpful. We also welcome your reaction to your child's report and any suggestions you may have for more effectively helping your child.

Comments, Reactions, Suggestions

1st Report:

We're very pleased with Julia's growth report and hope she continues to be a "pleasure." If we can help her with her reading, or in any other way, please let us know. (For the first time she is truly happy with her teacher—nice.)

Parent *Mrs. Thomas S. Taylor* Date *Nov. 27, 1954*

2nd Report:

We are very pleased with Julia's report. Will follow your suggestion to assist Julia in her reading development. We too have noted a bit of nervousness, but she appears to be outgrowing it.

Parent *Thomas S. Taylor* Date *14 Feb. 1955*

3rd Report: Dear Mr. Ponder — We too are very happy and proud of Julia's progress. This has been her most contented and happiest year in school. This we feel, has been due to your splendid teaching and the personal interest shown by you and Mrs. Even. We sincerely thank you.

Parent *Mr. & Mrs. Thomas S. Taylor* Date *16 May 1955*

177

Appendix B

MOTHER'S UNIVERSITY REPORT CARDS

University of Oregon
Fall, 1938-39
GRADE REPORT CARD

Student _Janice_ | _Louise_ | █████████
First Name | Middle Name | Last Name

Dept.	Course No.	Subject	Term Hours	Grade	Instructor
Psych	207	Elem Psych	3	C	Leeper
"	204	Psych Lab	1	C	Byrd
FN	211	Foods	3	C	Wood
Geo	105	Int. to Geog	3	B	Stovall
"	108	Geog Lab	1	B	Stovall
P.E.	111	El. Volley	1	B	Russell
P.S.	201	Am. Nat. Gov.	4	A	Schumaker

OVER

University of Oregon
U. of O.: Winter 1938-39
GRADE REPORT CARD

Student _Janice_ | _Louise_ | █████████
First Name | Middle Name | Last Name

Dept.	Course No.	Subject	Term Hours	Grade	Instructor
Pol. Sc.	202	Am. State & Local Govt	4	C	Schumaker
Psy.	208	Elem. Psy.	3	C	Leeper
Geog.	106	Intro Geog	3	B	Stovall
Geog.	109	Geog Lab	1	B	Staff
H.E.	217	Foods	3	B	Wood
Psy.	205	Elem. Psy Lab	1	C	Beal
P.E.	212	Old Fashioned Gim & Danc	1	A	Russell

OVER

178

Appendix C

Handout from 1988 class on "Personality Disorders;"
DSM-IV "Narcissistic Personality Disorder," Diagnostic Criteria,
Diagnostic and Statistical Manual of Mental Disorders 4th ed.,
American Psychiatric Association. (1994). [Electronic version].
Washington, D.C: Author. Retrieved December, 2005 from
http://www.behavenet.com/capsules/disorders/narcissisticpd.htm)

A. Behavior that is overly dramatic, reactive, and
    intensely expressed, as indicated by at least three
    of the following:

    (1) self-dramatization, e.g. exaggerated expression
        of emotions
    (2) incessant drawing of attention to oneself
    (3) craving for activity and excitement
    (4) overreaction to minor events
    (5) irrationa, angry outbursts or tantrums

B. Characteristic disturbances in interpersonal relation-
    ships as indicated by at least two of the following:

    (1) perceived by others as shallow and lacking
        genuineness, even if superficially warm and
        charming
    (2) egocentric, self-indulgent, and inconsiderate
        of others
    (3) vain and demanding
    (4) dependent, helpless, constantly seeking reassurance
    (5) prone to manipulative suicidal threats, gestures,
        or attempts

NARCISSISTIC PERSONALITY DISORDER

A. Grandiose sense of self-importance or uniqueness,
    e.g.,exaggeration of achievements and talents, focus
    on the special nature of one's problems.

B. Preoccupation with fantasies of unlimited success,
    power, brilliance, beauty or ideal love.

C. Exhibitionism: the person requires constant attention
    and admiration.

D. Cool indifference or marked feelings of rage, inferiority,
    shame, humiliation, or emptiness in response to criticism,
    indifference of others or defeat.

E. At least two of the following characteristic of disturbances
    in interpersonal relationships:

    (1) entitlement: expectation of special favors withot
        assuming reciprocal responsibilities, e.g., surprise
        and anger that people will not do what is wanted
    (2) interpersonal exploitativeness: taking advantage
        of others to indulge own desires or for self-aggrandizement;
        disregard for the personal integrity and rights
        of others
    (3) relationships that characteristically alternate
        between the extremes of overidealization and devaluation
    (4) lack of empathy; inability to recognize how others
        feel, e.g., unable to appreciate the distress of
        someone who is seriously ill.

BehaveNet® Clinical Capsule™:
DSM-IV & DSM-IV-TR:
Narcissistic Personality Disorder

Individuals with this Cluster B Personality Disorder have an excessive sense of how important they are. They demand and expect to be admired and praised by others and are limited in their capacity to appreciate others' perspectives.

Diagnostic criteria for 301.81 Narcissistic Personality Disorder
(cautionary statement)

A pervasive pattern of grandiosity (in fantasy or behavior), need for admiration, and lack of empathy, beginning by early adulthood and present in a variety of contexts, as indicated by five (or more) of the following:

(1) has a grandiose sense of self-importance (e.g., exaggerates achievements and talents, expects to be recognized as superior without commensurate achievements)

(2) is preoccupied with fantasies of unlimited success, power, brilliance, beauty, or ideal love

(3) believes that he or she is "special" and unique and can only be understood by, or should associate with, other special or high-status people (or institutions)

(4) requires excessive admiration

(5) has a sense of entitlement, i.e., unreasonable expectations of especially favorable treatment or automatic compliance with his or her expectations

(6) is interpersonally exploitative, i.e., takes advantage of others to achieve his or her own ends

(7) lacks empathy: is unwilling to recognize or identify with the feelings and needs of others

(8) is often envious of others or believes that others are envious of him or her

(9) shows arrogant, haughty behaviors or attitudes

Reprinted with permission from the Diagnostic and Statistical Manual of Mental Disorders, fourth Edition. Copyright 1994 American Psychiatric Association

---

Also: narcissism

Appendix D

"What to Watch for When Adults Play with Children," Blue Sky Bridge. Retrieved January, 2006 from http://www.blueskybridge. org/resource_adultsplayingwchildren.htm

Articles

Select Another Article ▼

What to Watch for When Adults Play with Children

Have you ever watched someone playing with a child and felt uncomfortable with it? Perhaps you thought, "I'm just overreacting," or, "He/She doesn't really mean that." Don't ignore the behavior; learn how to ask more questions about what you have seen. The following checklist offers some warning signs. Do you know an adult who:

- Refuses to let a child set any of his or her own limits?
- Insists on hugging, touching, kissing, tickling, wrestling with, or holding a child even when the child clearly does not want this affection?
- Is overly interested in the sexuality of a particular child or teen (e.g. talks repeatedly about the child's developing body or interferes with normal teen dating)?
- Manages to get time alone or insists on time alone with the child with no interruptions?
- Spends most of his or her spare time with children and has little interest in spending time with someone his or her own age?
- Regularly offers to baby-sit many different children for free or take children on overnight outings alone?
- Buys children expensive gifts or gives them money for no apparent reason?
- Frequently walks in on children or teens in the bathroom?
- Allows children or teens to consistently get away with inappropriate sexualized behaviors?

If you answered "yes" to some of these questions, talk to that person. If you are uncomfortable, but don't see the signs, be sure to trust your instincts and ask questions. For information and advice on how to talk to someone, please call Blue Sky Bridge at 303-444-1388. This information comes from the *National Child Advocate*, Vol. 5, No. 2.

References

"ASPCA HISTORY: 'REGARDING HENRY,'" The
American Society for the Prevention of Cruelty to
Animals. Retrieved April, 2005 from http://www.aspca.
org/site/PageServer?pagename=about_history

Bagley, C., Wood, M., and Young, L. (1994) Victim to abuser:
Mental health and behavioral sequels of child sexual abuse
in a community survey of young adult males. *Child Abuse
& Neglect,* 18, 683-697.

Bishop, Elizabeth. (2005, November 18). Former McClatchy
teacher sentenced to jail for statutory rape. *Sacramento
News 10.* Retrieved January, 2006 from http://www.news10.
net/printfullstory.aspx?storyid+14360

Bolton, F., Morris, L., and MacEachron, A. (1989) *Males at Risk:
The Other Side of Child Sexual Abuse.* Newbury Park, CA:
Sage Publications.

Brazelton, T. Berry M.D., Professor Emeritus of Pediatrics,
Harvard Medical School, quotation from Healthy Families
America. Retrieved April, 2005 from http://www.
healthyfamiliesamerica.org/quotations/index.shtml

"C. Henry Kempe," Who Named It? Retrieved April, 2005 from
http://www.whonamedit.com/doctor.cfm/861.htm

"Child Maltreatment 2003 Report," the 14th annual publication
of data collected via NCANDS, available at the U.S.
Department of Health and Human Services Children's

Bureau website. Retrieved March, 2005 from http://www.
acf.dhhs.gov/programs/cb/publications/cmreports.htm
and retrieved August 2006 from http://www.acf.hhs.gov/
programs/cb/pubs/cm03/index.htm

"Child Maltreatment 2003: Summary of Key Findings," National
Clearinghouse on Child Abuse and Neglect Information.
Retrieved March, 2005 from http://nccanch.acf.hhs.gov/
pubs/factsheets/canstats.cfm

Coronado, Ramon. (2005, July 7). Friends pleas for teacher in
student sex case. *Sacramento Bee.* Retrieved January, 2006
from http://www.sacbee.com/content/news/story/13190645p-
14033871c.html

Courtois, C. (1988). *Healing The Incest Wound: Adult Survivors
in Therapy.* New York: W.W. Norton & Company.

"Definitions of Child Abuse and Neglect," State Statutes Series
2005, National Clearinghouse on Child Abuse and Neglect
Information. Retrieved March, 2005 from http://nccanch.
acf.hhs.gov and retrieved August, 2006 from http://www.
childwelfare.gov/systemwide/laws_policies/statutes/
defineall.pdf

Diagnostic and Statistical Manual of Mental Disorders (3rd ed.),
American Psychiatric Association. (1980). Washington, D.C:
Author. Cited in typewritten handouts given to students
during a one-day course on "Personality Disorders," the
"NCA Winter School On Addictive Behavior," January 20,
1988; sponsored by the National Council on Alcoholism,
Mesa County Chapter, The Alcohol Council of Colorado,
in cooperation with The Alcohol and Drug Abuse Division,
Colorado Department of Health.

Diagnostic and Statistical Manual of Mental Disorders (4th
ed.), American Psychiatric Association. (1994). [Electronic
version]. Washington, D.C: Author. Retrieved December,

2005 from http://www.behavenet.com/capsules/disorders/
narcissisticpd.htm

"Fact Sheet: Sexual Abuse of Children from Prevent Child
Abuse America. Retrieved March, 2005 from http://
www.preventchildabuse.org/learn_more/research.
html and retrieved August, 2006 from http://member.
preventchildabuse.org/site/DocServer/sexual_abuse.pdf?
docID=126 at http://member.preventchildabuse.org/site/
PageServer?pagename=research_ fact_sheets

Falton, B., Lajoie, J., Trocme, N., Chaze, F., MacLaurin,
B., and Black, T. (2005). *Sexual abuse of children in
Canada*. CECW Information Sheet #25E. Montreal, QC:
McGill University, School of Social Work. Retrieved
February, 2006 from http://www.cecw-cepb.ca/DocsEng/
CISSexAbuse25E.pdf

"About the Federal Child Abuse Prevention and Treatment
Act," National Clearinghouse on Child Abuse and Neglect
Information. Retrieved March, 2005 from http://nccanch.
acf.hhs.gov and retrieved August, 2006 from http://www.
childwelfare.gov/pubs/factsheets/about.cfm

Finkelhor, D. (1984). *Child Sexual Abuse: New Theory and
Research*. New York: The Free Press.

Finkelhor, D. (1990). Early and long-term effects of child sexual
abuse: An update. *Professional Psychology: Research and
Practice, 21*, 325-330.

Finkelhor, D. (1994). "Current Information on the Scope and
Nature of Child Sexual Abuse" [Electronic version]. *The
Future of Children*, Full Journal Issue: Sexual Abuse of
Children, 4 (2): 31-53. Retrieved March, 2005 from http://
www.futureofchildren.org/information2826/information_
show.htm?doc id=74226

Freyd, J. J. (1996). *Betrayal Trauma: The Logic of Forgetting Childhood Abuse*. Cambridge, MA: Harvard University Press.

Healthy Families America Retrieved January, 2006 from http://www.healthyfamiliesamerica.org/downloads/hfa_facts_features.pdf http://www.healthyfamiliesamerica.org/about_us/index.shtml http://www.healthyfamiliesamerica.org/about_us/critical_elements.shtml

"How American Humane Began," American Humane. Retrieved April, 2005 from http://www.americanhumane.org/site/PageServer?pagename=wh_mission_ history

Jerard, Jessica. "Promoting Attachment in Adopted Infants." Families with Children from China. Retrieved January, 2006 from http://www.fccny.org/newsletter/?36#Promoting

MSN Encarta online dictionary: definition of "walking wounded." Retrieved January, 2006 from http://encarta.msn.com/dictionary_1861709537_1861709549/prevpage.html

Nicholson, Kieran. (2005, November 15). Mom gets 30 years for sex with boys. *Denver Post*. Retrieved January, 2006 from http://www.denverpost.com/portlet/article/html/fragments/print_article.jsp?article=3216381

"The NYSPCC Story," The New York Society for the Prevention of Cruelty to Children. Retrieved April, 2005 from http://www.nyspcc.org/beta_history/nyspcc_story.htm

"The Real Story of Mary Ellen Wilson," American Humane. Retrieved April, 2005 from http://www.americanhumane.org/site/PageServer?pagename=wh_mission_maryellen

"The Response," The New York Society for the Prevention of Cruelty to Children. Retrieved April, 2005 from http://www.nyspcc.org/beta_history/response.htm

Rosencrans, B. (1997). *The Last Secret: Daughters Sexually Abused by Mothers*. Brandon, Vermont: The Safer Society Press.

"Sexual Harassment: Title IX of The Education Amendments of 1972." U.S. Department of Education, Office for Civil Rights, Washington, D.C. Retrieved January, 2006 from http://www.mith2.umd.edu/WomensStudies/GenderIssues/ SexualHarassment/U MDManual/appendix-c

"Something About Amelia," made-for TV movie, 1984. Retrieved January, 2006 from the Internet Movie Database http://www.imdb.com/ and http://www.imdb. com/title/tt0088149/

"U. S. Navy Service and Campaign Medals" Retrieved (second retrieval) August, 2006 from http://www.history.navy. mil/medals/ with additional retrievals from http://www. gruntsmilitaryu.com/acpm.shtml http://www.history.navy. mil/medals/adsm.htm http://www.history.navy.mil/medals/ ww2vic.htm

Urquiza, A. (1988). The effects of childhood sexual abuse in an adult male population. University of Washington, Seattle. Doctoral dissertation.

"What is Child Abuse and Neglect?" National Clearinghouse on Child Abuse and Neglect Information. Retrieved March, 2005 http://nccanch.acf.hhs.gov and retrieved August, 2006 from http://www.childwelfare.gov/pubs/factsheets/ whatiscan.cfm

"What to Watch for When Adults Play with Children," Blue Sky Bridge. Retrieved January, 2006 from http://www. blueskybridge.org/resource_adultsplayingwchildren.htm

Bibliography

Brown, Nina W. (2001). *Children of the Self-Absorbed: A Grownup's Guide to Getting Over Narcissistic Parents.* Oakland, CA: New Harbinger Publications, Inc.

Crewdson, John (1988). *By Silence Betrayed: Sexual Abuse of Children in America.* New York: Harper & Row.

Elliott, Michele (Eds.) (1994). *Female Sexual Abuse of Children.* New York: The Guilford Press.

Farmer, Steven (1989). *Adult Children of Abusive Parents: A Healing Program for Those Who Have Been Physically, Sexually, or Emotionally Abused.* New York: Ballantine Books (RGA Publishing Group, Inc.).

Forward, Susan (1989). *Toxic Parents: Overcoming Their Hurtful Legacy and Reclaiming Your Life.* New York: Bantam Books.

Friel, John and Friel, Linda (1990). *An Adult Child's Guide to What Is "Normal."* Deerfield Beach, Florida: Health Communications, Inc.

Garbarino, James and Guttmann, Edna and Seeley, Janis Wilson. (1988). *The Psychologically Battered Child.* San Francisco, CA: Jossey-Bass Inc., Publishers.

Gartner, Richard B. (1999). *Betrayed As Boys: Psychodynamic Treatment of Sexually Abused Men.* New York: The Guilford Press.

Gartner, Richard B. (2005). *Beyond Betrayal: Taking Charge of Your Life after Boyhood Sexual Abuse*. Canada: John Wiley & Sons, Ltd.

Gasker, Janice A. (1999). *I Never Told Anyone This Before: Managing the Initial Disclosure of Sexual Abuse Recollections*. New York: Haworth Press.

Gil, Eliana M. (1983). Outgrowing the Pain: A Book for and about Adults *Abused As Children*. Walnut Creek, CA: Launch Press.

Herman, Judith Lewis. (1997). *Trauma and Recovery: The Aftermath of Violence—from Domestic Abuse to Political Terror*. New York: Basic Books.

Hislop, Julia (2001). *Female Sex Offenders: What Therapists, Law Enforcement and Child Protective Services Need to Know*. Ravensdale, Washington: Issues Press.

"Home Visitation Programs in New Jersey: A Promising Approach for Preventing Child Abuse and Neglect," Joint Workgroup of: The NJ Task Force on Child Abuse and Neglect and the Governor's Juvenile Justice and Delinquency Prevention Committee. (Nov. 30, 2004) Retrieved March, 2005 from http://www. preventchildabusenj.org/documents/index/HomeVisitation ProgramsinNJ113004.pdf

Hunter, Mic (1991). *Abused Boys: The Neglected Victims of Sexual Abuse*. New York: Ballantine Books.

Katz, Mark (1997). *On Playing A Poor Hand Well: Insights from the Lives of Those Who Have Overcome Childhood Risks and Adversities*. New York: W.W. Norton & Company.

Kertscher, Tom. (2000, June 30). Experts say mother-daughter incest is a hidden Crime. *Milwaukee Journal Sentinel*.

Retrieved January, 2006 from http://www.jsonline.com/
news/metro/jun00/incest30062900a.asp

Lambie, Glenn W. (2005). "Child Abuse and Neglect: A Practical
Guide for Professional School Counselors." *Professional
School Counseling*, 8 (3): 249-258. American School
Counselor Association.

Lew, Mike (2004). *Victims No Longer: The Classic Guide for
Men Recovering from Sexual Child Abuse*. New York:
HarperCollins.

Making Daughters Safe Again http://mdsasupport.homestead.
com/index.html

Miller, Alice (1981). *The Drama of the Gifted Child*. New York:
Basic Books.

Miller, Alice (1990). *Banished Knowledge: Facing Childhood
Injuries*. New York: Nan A. Talese.

Miller, Alice (2001). *The Truth Will Set You Free*. New York:
Basic Books.

Munro, Kali, M.Ed., Toronto psychotherapist http://www.
kalimunro.com/index.html http://www.kalimunro.com/
article_sexual_abuse_by_mothers.html

Ogilvie, Beverly A. (2004). *Mother-Daughter Incest A Guide
for Helping Professionals*. Binghamton, NY: The Haworth
Maltreatment and Trauma Press.

Peck, Scott M. (1983). *People of the Lie*. New York: Simon &
Schuster, Inc.

Pelzer, David J. (1995). *A Child Called "It:" An abused Child's
Journey from Victim to Victor*. Deerfield Beach, Florida:
Health Communications, Inc.

Pelzer, David J. (2001). *Help Yourself: Finding Hope, Courage, and Happiness.* New York: Plume.

Reckling, Anne E. (2004). "Mother-Daughter Incest: When Survivors Become Mothers" [Electronic version]. *Journal of Trauma Practice*, 3 (2): 49-71. Retrieved August, 2006 from http://www.haworthpressinc.com/

Salter, Anna C. (1995). *Transforming Trauma: A Guide to Understanding and Treating Adult Survivors of Child Sexual Abuse.* Thousand Oaks, CA: Sage Publications, Inc.

Southern Poverty Law Center http://www.splcenter.org/center/about.jsp The Southern Poverty Law Center was founded in 1971 as a small civil rights law firm. Today, the Center is internationally known for its tolerance education programs, its legal victories against white supremacists and its tracking of hate groups.

Tower, Cynthia Crosson (1988). *Secret Scars: A Guide for Survivors of Child Sexual Abuse.* New York: Penguin Books

Van Derbur, Marilyn (2003). *Miss America By Day: Lessons Learned From Ultimate Betrayals and Unconditional Love.* Denver, Colorado: Oak Hill Ridge Press.

Woititz, Janet Geringer (1989). *Healing Your Sexual Self.* Deerfield Beach, Florida: Health Communications, Inc.

Wolin, Steven J. and Wolin, Sybil. (1993). *The Resilient Self: How Survivors of Troubled Families Rise Above Adversity.* New York: Villard Books (Random House, Inc.).

Acknowledgments

Writing this book has been one of the most challenging yet gratifying undertakings of my life. But more than anything else, it has been humbling. Even on days I felt it hurt too much to keep writing, it seemed somehow my sacred obligation to tell the story that many others cannot. If not I, who?

I want to thank the people who helped me with this book—professionals, friends, and researchers—those who are advocates for victims, those who are fellow survivors of child sexual abuse and those who are both. Their support made all the difference:

- First always, my husband, best friend, and editor, Jeff, who would not let me abandon this project (even when I begged).

- Jennifer J. Freyd, Ph.D., Professor of Psychology, University of Oregon and Editor, *Journal of Trauma & Dissociation*, for her interest and encouragement.

- Harvard University Press for granting permission to reprint verbatim text excerpts from Freyd's book, *Betrayal Trauma*:

  Reprinted by permission of the publisher from BETRAYAL TRAUMA: THE LOGIC OF FORGETTING CHILDHOOD ABUSE by Jennifer J. Freyd, pp. 62-63; 75 Cambridge, Mass.: Harvard University Press, Copyright ©1996 by Jennifer Freyd.

- Kali Munro, M.Ed., EMDR II, Toronto Psychotherapist and Online Counselor (http://www.KaliMunro.com) who is affiliated with the organization, "Making Daughters Safe Again," (http://mdsasupport.homestead.com/2004/home.htm), whom

I first e-mailed back in 2004. Her enthusiastic response helped launch this project.

- Brian Luke Seaward, author, teacher, speaker, whom I met when I attended a 2005 writers' workshop at the University of Colorado in Boulder. His session on writing nonfiction was most helpful. Even more inspiring were his genuineness and positive energy. (http://www.brianlukeseaward.net/)

- David Finkelhor, Ph.D., the Director of the Crimes against Children Research Center, Co-Director of the Family Research Laboratory and Professor of Sociology at the University of New Hampshire, whom I also e-mailed, initially in 2004. (http://www.unh.edu/ccrc/) He gave me specific resources to explore and also granted me permission to cite his work.

The remaining acknowledgments are more personal. I am thankful for the many angels in my life. Because they may not wish to be openly recognized I will not use their names. They include:

Teachers—from elementary school years through graduate school—who made school a safe haven for me and for so many others.

Ministers—at Willamette University, Salem, Oregon and First Methodist Church, Eugene, Oregon; a youth church camp director and his wife, summer, 1966; my dear friend and former minister in the Midwest.

A few of my parents' friends whose kind words ("It must have been difficult growing up in your household.") were small affirmations that helped save my sanity.

My maternal grandfather and my mother's brother and his family, who were never anything but kind to me.

My wonderful adult children and stepchildren.

My dear women friends—from high school and college and beyond—my "sisters of the heart."

and

Other sexual abuse survivors who have shared their stories, their strength and their resiliency with me.

Thank you.

Bless you all.
Julie

About the Author

JULIE A. BRAND, M.S.

Julie holds a Master's degree in Counseling and Guidance and enjoyed a distinguished 25-year career as a school counselor. Newly retired, she now uses her unique perspective as both an experienced counselor and a resilient survivor of maternal incest to write and to speak about mother-daughter sexual abuse.

In 2006, she founded C.A.P.E.R. Consulting: Child Abuse Prevention, Education and Recovery. Visit her web site at: http://www.caperconsulting.com/

Married to Jeff since 1994, they live in Longmont, Colorado with their mostly golden retriever, Murrey. Between them they have four sons, one daughter, one daughter-in-law and one grandson.

In her book and in her workshops, Julie combines research data, professional expertise and her personal experiences to enlighten audiences about the existence of mother-daughter sexual abuse. Her goals are to empower child welfare professionals—from first responders to therapists—to recognize the dynamics of maternal incest, to intervene and to help victims become strong, healthy adults. The cycle of child abuse *can* be broken.

Lightning Source UK Ltd.
Milton Keynes UK
26 July 2010
157472UK00002B/58/A